Eyewitness Accounts of the American Revolution

Memoir and Letters of Captain W. Glanville Evelyn
Edited by G. D. Scull

The New York Times & Arno Press

Reprint Edition 1971 by Arno Press Inc.

*

LC# 71-140882
ISBN 0-405-01209-8

*

Eyewitness Accounts of the American Revolution, Series III
ISBN for complete set: 0-405-01187-3

*

Manufactured in the United States of America

MEMOIR AND LETTERS

OF

WILLIAM GLANVILLE EVELYN.

I am, My Dear Madam,
Your dutifull & Affec.te Son
W. G. Evelyn
New York Island Sep.t 25.th 1776

MEMOIR AND LETTERS

OF

CAPTAIN W. GLANVILLE EVELYN,

OF THE 4TH REGIMENT, ("KING'S OWN,")

FROM

North America, 1774—1776.

EDITED AND ANNOTATED BY

G. D. SCULL,

MEMBER OF THE ACADEMY OF NATURAL SCIENCES OF PHILADELPHIA, THE HISTORICAL SOCIETY OF PENNSYLVANIA, THE NEW ENGLAND HISTORIC, GENEALOGICAL SOCIETY OF BOSTON, AND THE HARLEIAN SOCIETY OF LONDON.

Printed for Private Circulation by
JAMES PARKER AND CO., OXFORD.
1879.

PREFACE.

THE old family seat of Wotton House, once the residence of the celebrated John Evelyn, author of "Sylva," is now in the possession of his collateral kinsman, William John Evelyn, Esq. Here are still preserved the MSS. of the well-known diary, several portraits of John Evelyn and his wife, and their descendants, the Prayer-Book used by Charles I. on the scaffold, and many other most interesting relics of that period. During a visit to Wotton, made by the Editor of this little volume in 1877, he ascertained that some letters, written by Mr. Evelyn's grand-uncle, Capt. William Glanville Evelyn, were still in existence, and in the possession of the family. These letters, sixteen in number, were written from the seat of war in North America, during the early years of the Revolution, to Captain Evelyn's relations in Ireland and Great Britain. They were found to be somewhat dilapidated, and fast going to decay, and it was suggested to Mr. Evelyn by the Editor, that they should be copied and printed, with full notes, and a slight memoir of the writer, drawn up from the very scanty materials still remaining. Mr. Evelyn, in the kindest and most obliging manner (amidst the urgency of his own private affairs), made careful copies himself of all the original letters, and placed them in the hands of the Editor, for private publication. He has taken much pains to elucidate the text with notes, drawn from many sources. Mr. Evelyn has also rendered the Editor much valuable assistance.

Some particulars relating to the death of Capt. Evelyn, were related to the present owner of Wotton more than thirty years ago, by Mr. Daniel Webb Webber, of Dublin, who knew Capt. Evelyn personally, and was indeed a distant connexion of his family.

About two years ago, an inquiry was started to ascertain the place of burial of the writer of these letters in New York. Nothing definite could be ascertained beyond the fact, that "an English officer was interred during the month of October, 1776, in the ground of the Lutheran church on Broadway." For their zealous and able assistance in this inquiry, the thanks of both Mr. Evelyn and myself are particularly due to Mr. T. Baily Myers, of New York, to Mr. William Kelby, assistant-librarian to the New York Historical Society,

Mr. Spofford, of the Congressional Library at Washington, Mr. Benson J. Lossing, Mr. William John Potts, of Camden, New Jersey, and to Mr. Benjamin D. Hicks, of old Westbury, Long Island.

I am also indebted for much valuable information, drawn through Mr. W. J. Potts, to the following gentlemen :—Rev. Charles W. Baird, of Rye, New York, Mr. Henry B. Dawson, of Morrisiania, Mr. Isaac P. Greenwood, and Mr. Henry P. Johnston (author of the "Campaign of 1776 around New York and Brooklyn"), and to Mr. Edward F. Delancey, of New York. To Miss Elizabeth Ellery Dana, of Boston, my thanks are due for extracts from the unpublished parts of the "Journal of a British Officer in America." Mr. W. J. Potts has our especial thanks for most valuable assistance, rendered during the inquiry concerning the military career of Captain Evelyn in America, and for much important information furnished to me by him. To Mr. Charles R. Hildeburn, of Philadelphia, I also desire to express our obligations, for an interesting extract from the MS. journal of his great-grandfather, Lieutenant George Inman, who was the comrade and friend of Capt. W. G. Evelyn.

Captain A. E. Lawson Lowe, of Nottingham, has favoured me with some notes from his collection of genealogical papers, and Mr. Joseph W. Drexel, of New York, has, in the kindest manner, placed at my disposal several photographs of rare engravings in his collection.

Col. E. W. Vernon Harcourt, of Nuneham Park, with most obliging courtesy, has also sent photographs of a rare print, and allowed me to copy the letters written by Lieutenant-Colonel William Harcourt, to his father, Earl Harcourt, during the years 1776 and 1777, from the seat of war in North America.

G. D. SCULL.

Rugby, August 13, 1879.

CONTENTS.

	PAGE
MEMOIR	1
Extract from the Official Records of the 4th Regiment	13
ROBERT EVELIN	15
His descendants	25

LETTERS OF CAPTAIN W. G. EVELYN.

I. To his Father	26
II. To the Hon. Mrs. Leveson Gower . .	29
III. To the same	31
IV. To his Father	38
V. To the Hon. Mrs. Leveson Gower . .	41
VI. To his Father	45
VII. To the same	53
English Account of the Battles of Lexington and Concord	56
VIII. To the Hon. Mrs. Leveson Gower . .	58
IX. To the same	63
X. To his Father	66
XI. To the same	68
XII. To the same	71
XIII. To the Hon. Mrs. Leveson Gower . .	76
XIV. To his Father	81
XV. To the Hon. Mrs. Boscawen . . .	83
XVI. To his Mother	88
Copy of the Will of Captain W. G. Evelyn . .	90
Memorandums	92

CONTENTS.

	PAGE
LETTER OF ENSIGN EVELYN TO HIS FATHER	95
APPENDIX	98
Col. Cleaveland	ib.
Brigadier-General Richard Prescott	100
Capture of General Charles Lee by Lieutenant-Colonel Harcourt	103
Extracts from "Memoirs of General James Wilkinson"	113
Edward Thoroton Gould	119
Trial of Rev. John Horne (Tooke)	124
Hugh, Earl Percy	126
The Hon. Mr. Boscawen	131
List of Officers serving in the 4th Foot, in 1776	133
Genealogical table to illustrate Capt. Evelyn's letters	135
INDEX	136

LIST OF AUTOTYPE PORTRAITS.

CAPT. W. G. EVELYN	*Frontispiece*	
JOHN EVELYN, ESQ.	*Facing p.*	12
THE HON. MRS. BOSCAWEN	,,	83
BRIG.-GEN. R. PRESCOTT	,,	100
RT. HON. WM. HARCOURT	,,	102
GEN. CHARLES LEE	,,	104
SIMON, EARL HARCOURT	,,	109
HUGH, EARL PERCY	,,	126

MEMOIR.

THE writer of the following Letters, William Glanville Evelyn, eldest son and heir of the Rev. William Evelyn, (afterwards Dean of Emley, and Vicar of Trim, Ireland), could claim to be of good extraction both on his father's and mother's side. Through his father, he was sixth in direct descent from George Evelyn, Esq., who (dying in 1603) was the common ancestor of three branches of the Evelyn family, settled at Long-Ditton, Godstone, and Wotton, in the county of Surrey. The Long-Ditton branch became extinct in the male line in 1692. The father of William belonged to the second, or Godstone branch of the family, and John Evelyn[a], the distinguished author of "Sylva,"

---

[a] John Evelyn, the son of Richard Evelyn, of Wotton, was born Oct. 31, 1620. He spent a number of years in France and other parts of Europe. In 1647 he married the daughter (then only fourteen) of Sir Richard Brown, the British resident at the Court of France, and settled permanently (in 1651-2) at Say's Court, near Deptford, Kent, formerly the property of his wife's father. Here he resided until May, 1694, when he removed to Wotton House. Say's Court was occupied by Peter the Great, as Mr. Evelyn's tenant in 1698, for three months: the Czar frequenting the King's Dockyard as a common workman, in order to learn the art of ship-building. Evelyn succeeded to the Wotton Estate on the death of his elder brother George, Oct. 4, 1699.

to the third or youngest branch, settled at Wotton. John Evelyn, in his Diary, several times mentions his kinsman, Sir John Evelyn of Godstone, Knight, who was a direct ancestor of William Glanville Evelyn, and who was, like John Evelyn, a grandson of the above George Evelyn, the common ancestor.

It appears from the Diary that on Feb. 11, 1649, John Evelyn dined with his kinsman at Westminster. In one edition of the Diary, the name is misprinted Sir Joseph Evelyn; but in the original MS. preserved at Wotton, it is clearly written "Sir Jo. Evelyn." This was Sir John Evelyn of

(Disraeli makes one of his characters say in "Lothair,"—"You should read Evelyn's 'Sylva.' Evelyn was a man who was almost perfection.") He wrote books and treatises on History, Art, both Painting and Sculpture, Engraving, having himself engraved five prints of his journey from Rome to Naples, and one of Wotton House. He had been instructed by Prince Rupert in his new art of Mezzotint. He also wrote on domestic and political economy, physical geography, forest-trees, ancient and modern architecture, horticulture, gardening, science, commerce, law and other subjects; in fact, they embraced well-nigh the whole round of human knowledge of that day. He is perhaps best known by his "Sylva," a discourse on forest-trees, and his Diary (almost as famous as that of his friend, Samuel Pepys), which he kept from the year 1641 to 1705. In character he was pure and blameless, amidst the profligate courtiers of Charles II. He was among them, but not of them, and was an object of affection and respect wherever he was known. He died in London, Feb. 27, 1705-6, aged eighty-six, and was buried in the family chapel at Wotton. By his direction the following maxim was inscribed on his tombstone:—

"That all is vanity which is not honest, and that there is no solid Wisdom but in real piety."

Godstone, who at that time represented the borough of Bletchingley, Surrey, in Parliament, and should not be confounded with his nephew, Sir John Evelyn of Wilts, M.P. for Ludgershall, who had been declared a traitor by Charles I. (See Clarendon, Ludlow, and the other histories of the period.)

There is another mention in the Diary of Sir John Evelyn of Godstone, July 2, 1649; on which day John Evelyn, being on a visit to his brother at Wotton, went from Wotton to visit Sir John Evelyn at Godstone. There he met also Sir John Evelyn of Wilts, the so-called traitor; and after leaving Godstone, returned to his residence at Say's Court, Deptford. In the Diary is the following entry, copied from the original MS. at Wotton, recording the birth of his third son, John, at Say's Court, Jan. 19, 1654-5 :—

"About $\frac{1}{2}$ after 10 in the morning was my wife delivered of another son, being my third, but 2nd living. Benedictus sit Deus in donis suis."

The following baptismal certificate, in John Evelyn's own handwriting (preserved at Wotton, but much injured by damp), shews that this son was christened at Say's Court on the 26th of January, and that Sir John Evelyn of Godstone was godfather (susceptor) on the occasion.

"John Evelyn, my 3rd son, was born at Say's Court, in the Parish of Deptford, in the County of Kent, on the xix of January 165⅘, and was christened the xxvi.

Susceptors, Sir John Evelyn, of Godstone in Surrey,
Lady Gerrard.
Officiating, Dr. Owen, ... tham, in ye chamber over the west Parlour.

Ita testor
J. EVELYN."

The Diary mentions that on Aug. 3, 1658, John Evelyn visited his cousin Sir John at Godstone, and that on Nov. 24, 1659, he again was the guest of his kinsman on the celebration of Sir John's forty-first wedding-day. The last mention of Sir John in the Diary is dated Oct. 14, 1677, on which day John Evelyn went to see "old Sir John Evelyn's Dormitory" at Godstone Church, "paved with marble where he and his lady lie, on a very stately monument at length, he in armour of white marble." This monument still exists.

Sir John was buried in the family vault at Godstone, Jan. 18, 1664. Sir John Evelyn's second son, George Evelyn, Esq., of Nutfield, near Godstone, is also referred to in Evelyn's Memoirs. This George Evelyn (grandfather of William, dean of Emley, and great-grandfather of Captain William Glanville Evelyn), was not only a kinsman, but, like his father, a friend of John Evelyn, author of "Sylva."—(See Diary, March 30, 1694; Aug. 4, 1694; Feb. 20, 1695; June 19, 1699.)

George Evelyn of Nutfield, heir to his brother, Sir John Evelyn of Godstone, Baronet, (who died without male issue, Aug., 1671) was a deputy-lieutenant of Surrey, and was thrice elected Member of Parliament for the borough of Bletchingley, which his father, Sir John Evelyn of Godstone, had also represented.

There is in Evelyn's Diary an interesting account of a visit of John Evelyn to his cousin, Aug. 4, 1694 :—

"I went to visit my cousin, George Evelyn of Nutfield, where I found 10 children, 5 sons and 5 daughters. All painted in one piece very well by Mr. Lutterell, in crayon on copper. The boys were at school."

This picture, by Henry Lutterell, is now at Wotton. Of the five sons of George Evelyn here mentioned, Richard, the fourth son, was grandfather of Captain William Glanville Evelyn.

Little did John Evelyn foresee, when he paid this visit to his kinsman, that his own branch of the family would become extinct, and that a descendant of his kinsman would succeed to the family estate of Wotton. George Evelyn, of Nutfield, was born Dec. 4, 1641; died June 19, 1699; and was buried in the family vault at Godstone, June 24, 1699. The last allusion to him in Evelyn's Diary, is dated June 19, 1699 : "My cousin, George Evelyn of Nutfield, died suddenly." He should be distinguished from his kinsman, Captain George Evelyn "the great traveller," mentioned in Evelyn's Diary Feb. 26, 1649, and June 8, 1652, at which latter date George Evelyn of Nutfield would have been but in his eleventh year.

At Wotton there are portraits of Sir John Evelyn of Godstone, of his son George of Nutfield, and also of John Evelyn, grandfather of the present head of the family, and brother of Captain William Glanville Evelyn, of whom, it is much to be regretted, no full-sized portrait exists at Wotton.

The above extracts from Evelyn's Diary have been here introduced to shew the intimacy which existed between the author of "Sylva" and the ancestors of Captain William Glanville Evelyn. He was born at Arklow, county Wicklow, Ireland, early in 1742. His mother was the daughter of Christopher Chamberlain, Esq., of Chamberlainstown, co. Meath; the Chamberlains[b] being a very ancient and honourable family, who once held considerable possessions in the county of Meath. At the age of eighteen, through the interest of his English connections, he obtained an ensigncy in the 50th Regiment of Foot; and his first commission bears date

[b] This family is alluded to by Edmund Spenser, the Elizabethan poet, in his "View of the state of Ireland," where he mentions that in the year 1316, "Edward le Bruce, in his invasion of Ireland, rooted out the noble families of Audlies, Tuchets, *Chamberlaines*, Maundevilles, and the Savages out of Ardes." The family of Chamberlain is now represented by Tankerville Chamberlain, Esq., Barrister-at-law.

March 29, 1760. At that time the contest between England and France concerning their American possessions, had led both Powers to seek allies on the European Continent, and England found an ally in Prussia, France in Austria; Prussia and Austria being then engaged in the "seven-years' war [c]." In this continental struggle [d] the young officer, serving with his regiment, received what has been called the "baptism of fire;" but England withdrawing from the war, on the signing of the treaty of Fontainebleau at Paris, peace was proclaimed in London on March 22, 1763, and the 50th regiment, with the others, was reduced to a peace establishment. The troops were recalled, and William Evelyn, who held then the rank of lieutenant, retired on half-pay. After passing some years at home with his parents in the county of Antrim, in 1767, (July 16), he was re-appointed into the 4th or King's Own regiment [e], and attained the rank of

[c] "When, therefore, war between the two countries seemed inevitable, an augmentation was made to the army, and in December, 1755, eleven regiments of infantry were raised, which have been since retained, and are numbered from the 50th to the 60th inclusive."—*Moorsum's Historical Record of the 52nd Regiment.* 1860.

[d] See letter of his, written at this date, placed after the Letters.

[e] This celebrated corps was raised by Royal authority, on July 13, 1680, and was called the 2nd Tangier Regiment. In 1684 Charles II. conferred upon it the title of " Her Royal Highness the Duchess of York and Albany's Regiment, or the Queen's Regiment of Foot." In 1703 it became a Marine corps, and was called "the Queen's Regiment of Marines." In 1715 it was stationed at Windsor, when George I. conferred upon it the title of the King's Own, which it most

Captain, October 16, 1772. This regiment being one of those engaged in the American War of Independence, William Evelyn was again destined to see active service in the field. In company with his cousin, George Evelyn Boscawen (aged seventeen), for whom an ensigncy had been procured, he embarked for Boston to join his regiment, where he arrived in June, 1774.

In the preceding month (May 17, 1774), General Gage had landed in Boston on his mission of coercion from George III. Bancroft says that Gage lacked the necessary firmness for the occasion, for

"he had promised the king that with 4 regiments he would play the 'lion;' and troops beyond his requisitions were hourly expected. His injunctions enjoined upon him the seizure and condign punishment of Samuel Adams, Hancock, Joseph Warren, and other leading patriots, but he stood in such dread of them, that he never so much as attempted their arrest."

The general congress of delegates from all the colonies or States met at Philadelphia Sept. 1, 1774. The first collision between the British and American troops took place in Massachusets in Feb. 1775. Within a few weeks thereafter, the first actual conflict in arms occurred at Lexington and Concord, (April 19). Both Captain Evelyn and young Ensign

honourably bears to this day. The record of this very distinguished corps is surpassed by none in the British army, or any other, for long and most gallant services in almost every quarter of the globe.

WILLIAM GLANVILLE EVELYN. 9

Boscawen participated in these affairs, which are vividly described in the Letters. The next month (May), Forts Ticonderoga and Crown Point, on Lake Champlain, were taken by a party from Connecticut and Vermont. The next (June 17), the battle of Bunker Hill, near Boston, was fought, to the nominal advantage of the British, but to the real advantage of the Americans. Two days before this battle, George Washington was commissioned by the Continental Congress as Commander-in-chief of the Continental army, and issued his first order to the "United Provinces of North America" on July 14. In August, 1775, Washington was closely investing Boston, and early in March, 1776, that city was evacuated by the British. After refitting at Halifax, they moved on to New York. On July 12, Lord Howe reached Staten Island, and the troops of Clinton and Cornwallis arrived on Aug. 1, followed eleven days later by 11,000 Hessians and English. On Aug. 27, the battle of Long Island was fought, which ended in the abandonment of Long Island to the British, and in the subsequent entry of their troops into New York.

General Howe says, in his "Despatch to Lord George Germaine, of Nov. 30, 1776:"—

"On the 18th (Oct.) several corps re-imbarked in flat boats, and passing round Frog's Neck (Throck's or Throg's), landed on Pell's point at the mouth of Hutchinson's river; after which the main body crossed the mouth of that river to the same place, advanced immediately, and laid that night upon their arms, with the left upon a creek opposite to East Chester, and the right near to Rochelle. On the march to this ground, a skirmish ensued with a small party of the enemy posted to defend a narrow causeway, who were pursued for a mile, when a considerable body appearing in front, behind the "Bendstone" stone walls and in woods, some companies of light infantry, and a part of the chasseurs, were detached to dislodge them, which they did effectually: Lieutenant Colonel Musgrave commanding the 1st battalion of Light Infantry, and *Captain Evelyn* of the 4th Regiment, were both wounded; the latter is since dead, and much to be regretted as a gallant officer, but Lieutenant Colonel Musgrave is in a fair way of recovery: three soldiers were killed and twenty wounded."

Dr. Stiles[f], in his Diary, mentions that he was an eye-witness of the above skirmish, and says in a letter of Oct. 19, 1776, that there was an "unexpected fire" from Colonel Shepherd's regiment, and then "a second and third, which broke the enemy so much, that they ran away as fast as they could in confusion;" though, as General Heath observes in his Memoirs, "being immediately supported, they returned vigorously to the charge."

It would appear that Captain Evelyn was well in advance of his company, and that after he had

---

[f] Ezra Stiles, D.D., LL.D., born at New Haven, Connecticut, 1727; President of Yale College from 1777 until his death in 1795. The MS. diary is in the possession of Yale College.

vaulted over the wall, and whilst he lay wounded (apparently dead), the retreat commenced. For Colonel Glover, the American officer in command, writing from the camp at Mile Square, Oct. 22, states, that the constant fire

"caused them to retreat several times, once in particular, so far, that *a soldier of Colonel Shepherd's leaped over the wall and took a hat and a canteen off a Captain that lay dead on the ground* they retreated from."

According to the account preserved in the family, Captain Evelyn, after vaulting over the stone wall, had not proceeded far when he received three bullet-shots: the first grazed his left arm, the second inflicted a wound on the upper part of the thigh, the third shattered the right leg above the knee. Timely amputation might have saved his life, but he would not consent to the operation until it was too late. It was then performed in vain; and after lingering for nearly three weeks, he died at New York on Nov. 6, 1776. It is supposed that he was buried in the ground attached to Trinity Church, New York.

His character is to be traced in his Letters. Note his strong feelings of patriotism, his eagerness for opportunities of distinguishing himself, his affection for his friends at home, his tenderness and care for young Boscawen his kinsman, and his zealous regard for his duty, in refusing to exchange into a regiment going home when he had an opportunity.

The despatch of Sir William Howe, of Nov. 30, 1776, and the extract from the official records of the 4th, or King's Own Regiment, attest his value as an officer. Some allowance must be made for his strong prejudices against the American nation.

In the family account of him, he is said to have been

"a great loss to his Majesty's service,—of ardent spirit, zeal and talent for his profession, of a lively conversation and wit, of a warm and generous character, particularly well made—5 feet 10 inches in height, with dark eyes, features slightly marked with the small-pox."

He was never married, and his premature death was a great calamity to his family. Had he lived he would have become the head of the family of Evelyn. Owing to his untimely death, his brother John finally occupied this position, on the death of James Evelyn of Felbridge, Surrey, LL.D., in 1793, without male issue; and afterwards succeeded to the Wotton estates, as the devisee of Lady Evelyn, who died Nov. 12, 1817; she being the widow of Sir Frederick Evelyn, third Baronet, who died April 1, 1812, without male issue, and who represented the younger, or Wotton branch of the family.

JOHN EVELYN ESQ.RE
BORN AT ARKLOW, CO WICKLOW, IRELAND. 1ST JUNE 1743
DIED AT WOTTON, SURREY. 27TH NOVR 1827.
FROM A MINIATURE AT WOTTON 1784.

Extract from the Official Records of the 4th, or King's Own Regiment.

1776. "The King's Own were engaged in the movements by which General Washington was forced to abandon New York, which city was immediately taken possession of by the British General [g]. Washington having taken up a position in another part of the country, the British troops were again embarked in flat-bottomed boats, and landed near West Chester. Thence, re-embarking on the 18th of October, passed Throg's Neck, and landed at Pell's-point, at the mouth of Hutchinson's river. Advancing from thence, the troops encountered a detachment of provincials: a sharp skirmish ensued, in which several men were killed and wounded; and the

---

[g] From London Chronicle and London Gazette for December, 1776. "The accounts which have been received of the late operations of his Majesty's forces are to the following effect :—

"That on the 12th of October, the Guards, Light Infantry, and Reserve, together with Col. Dunop's corps of Hessian Grenadiers and Chasseurs, marched from the advanced posts on New York island; and embarking in boats at Turtle Bay, passed up the East river, through Hell Gate, and landed on Frog's (Throg's) Neck. That having crossed the neck, they found the bridge, which joined it to the main, had been broken down by the rebels, who had thrown up some works on the opposite side. That being joined by the 1st, 2nd, and 6th Brigades from Long Island, the troops embarked again in boats, and landed in Pelham's manor the 18th, without opposition; and marching through a random fire of the rebels from *Bendstone* walls, gained the road which leads from Connecticut to King's Bridge. The rebels, apprehending their communication to the eastward would be cut off, moved from their camp at King's Bridge, and extended their left to the White Plains, a chain of stoney hills so called. On the 21st, his Majesty's light troops took possession of the heights of New Rochelle. Col. Rogers with his New York companies, having taken post at Maramack (Mamaronack), was attacked by a party of rebels, which he drove back with considerable loss."

King's Own lost a most valuable and gallant officer, Captain W. Glanville Evelyn, who was mortally wounded, and whose fall was much regretted."

The following extracts are taken from the MS. Journal of George Inman, now in the possession of his great-grandson, Mr. Charles R. Hildeburn, of Philadelphia :—

"In December 1775, I attached myself to the Light Company of the 4th, or King's Own Regiment, commanded by my friend Captain Evelyn."

1776. "In October, part of the army embarked near Hell Gate, and proceeded for New Rochelle, near which my good and gallant friend received his mortal wound; and being carried to New York, soon expired, to the great regret of all that knew him as a soldier or friend."

ROBERT EVELIN.

ROBERT EVELIN, a younger son of George Evelin (or Evelyn) of Wotton, Surrey, emigrated to Virginia before the year 1610. Somewhat later he was followed by his son, also named Robert, and it is doubtless this Robert Evelin the younger to whom we must attribute the authorship of a series of Letters describing the new country, with the view of attracting emigrants thither. In this enterprise Robert the younger was associated with his maternal Uncle Young. He returned home in 1637, published his Letters, then after a time re-crossed the Atlantic, and is said to have "died in the West Indies."

In the year 1631[a], Charles I. made Sir Edmund Ployden a grant of all the territory now included in the State of New Jersey (United States), utterly disregarding a prior grant of a large portion thereof to the New England Company. This concession also included all the land now comprised in the State of Delaware, and parts of Maryland, Pennsyl-

---

[a] This account of the settlement of New Albion, is condensed from a rare little work published in Philadelphia in 1845, entitled "Reminiscences of Old Gloucester," New Jersey, by Isaac Mickle.

vania, and New York. With this grant, and a very liberal charter, was coupled the privilege of Sir Edmund Ployden's using the high-sounding title of Earl Palatine; and he was allowed to call his principality in the wilderness "New Albion." The rampant spirit of democracy in England during the reign of Charles I., had unsettled the minds of many rank royalists, and amongst them, none were more so than a certain Beauchamp Plantagenet, who claimed a lineal descent from the royal family of that name. This recent grant to Ployden opened to him an asylum whereby he could escape from the democratic evils which he thought menaced him.

He consulted with seven knights, his kinsmen and neighbours, and after numerous conferences with Ployden, it was agreed to send Plantagenet out to New Albion, as being "the oldest and boldest traveller." He was to visit all parts of Sir Edmund's territory, and to select the best place for the eight knights and gentlemen themselves, a hundred servants, and twenty of their old tenants and their families. They went over in the year 1636, and Plantagenet selected the country lying on the river Delaware, having ascended it sixty miles. He was instructed by Ployden to adhere to Cato's three cardinal rules of colonization, viz., "to secure a pure air, a fresh navigable river, and a rich country."

Certain of Plantagenet's countrymen had already

preceded him on the banks of this river, from Virginia, and built a fort, where they waited in patient expectation of meeting Ployden himself, who, however, did not arrive until some time before 1641. These Virginia settlers were Captain Young, his nephew, the famous Robert Evelin, and thirteen other traders, who arrived in 1633. At this post, the exact site of which is now lost, Evelin and his uncle kept up a trade with the Indians for four years. The various Indian tribes on the east of the Delaware were at that time "in several factions and wars against the Susquehannocks." Evelin describes them "as extream fearfull of a gun, naked and unarmed against our short swords and picks;" and adds, "I had some bickering with them, but they are of so little esteem, as I durst, with fifteen men, sit down or trade in despight of them." In the year 1637, Evelin, tired of waiting for the advent of Sir Edmund Ployden, returned to England, where he wrote a letter to the wife of Sir Edmund, urging her husband to go and take with him to America "three hundred men or more, as there is no doubt but that he may doe very well, and grow rich."

In 1637 also appeared the first part of Plantagenet's description of New Albion, the glowing accounts of which no doubt hastened the preparations of the Earl Palatine to visit his possessions. In anticipation of his coming, the wilderness was divided into baronies, and laid out into manorial tracts; all the Earl's children received titles, and a chivalric order was instituted, called "The Albion Knights of the Conversion," which had for its main object the conversion of the twenty-three kings, or sachems, of the Indian tribes. Hence, upon their badge we find the arms of the order impaling those of Ployden, supported by the right hand of a kneeling Indian, around which are twenty-three crowned heads, the whole being encircled by the motto, "Docebo iniquos vias tuas et impii ad te convertentur." The knight's device was a hand holding a crown upon the point of a dagger, above an open Bible, impaled with the arms of the Palatine, which were, On a field, or, two flowers proper, upon the points of a fesse indented, gules, and having as Motto, "Virtus beat sic suos." And as supporters, two stags, statant.

The Earl's favourite daughter, Lady Barbara, "the mirror of wit and beauty," was created Baroness of Richneck, so named from the fertility of the soil she owned. This property was "twenty-four miles compasse, of wood, huge timber-trees, and two feet black mould, much desired by the Virginians to plant tobacco." Bolalmanack, or Belvedere, on the shores of the Chesapeake, of the State of Delaware, was given to Plantagenet under the lord's seal, as a reward for his pains in exploring the country.

Robert Evelin.

After the arrival of the Earl Palatine in New Albion, about 1641, he and Plantagenet remained seven years, during which time they "marched, lodged, and cabinned amongst the Indians."

They were, however, unable to induce the requisite number (3,000) of "able trained men" to leave England, which had been promised them, and the project was ultimately abandoned; not, however, without another effort being made, in 1648, when Plantagenet's book was revised, and another edition issued.

The last edition of Robert Evelin's pamphlet appeared in 1648, with this long descriptive title:—

"A Description of the Province of New Albion, and a Direction for Adventurers with small stock to get two for one, and good land freely; and for gentlemen, and all Servants, Labourers, and Artificers to live plentifully. And a former discription re-printed of the healthiest, pleasantest, and richest Plantation of New Albion in North Virginia, proved by thirteen witnesses. Together with a Letter from Master Robert Evelin, that lived there many years, shewing the particularities and excellency thereof. With a briefe of the charge of victuall and necessaries to transport and buy stock for each Planter or Labourer, and how to get his Master £50 per annum or more, in 12 trades at £10 charge only a man."

This little book has become one of the very rarest of all the works on the early settlement of America. Allibone, in his "Dictionary of English and American Authors," calls it "liber rarissimus."

In the northern chancel of Wotton Church there is an alabaster monument to the memory of George Evelyn, Esq., the first of his family who resided at Wotton. Beneath the effigies of this George Evelyn and his two wives, is a group representing his twenty-four children. The first four figures in the group represent the four sons who survived him,— Thomas, John, and Robert, by his first wife, and Richard by his second.

To these four sons he left estates in the county of Surrey; Richard, the youngest, succeeded to Wotton, and became the father of the celebrated John Evelyn.

The male descendants of Thomas, the eldest, became extinct in 1692. John, the second son, is the direct ancestor of the present representative of the Evelyn family. It is of Robert, the third son, that we now proceed to give some account, though the materials are very scanty.

He was probably born at Long Ditton, in Surrey, about 1570. His mother, Rose (daughter and heiress of Thomas Williams, brother and heir of Sir John Williams, Knight), was buried at Long Ditton, July 21, 1577. In 1598, Queen Elizabeth granted a patent for making gunpowder, digging for saltpetre, &c., to John Evelyn, Robert Evelyn, and others, on condition of delivering at the Tower of London a certain number of lasts annually.

On the death of his father George, (who died

May 29, 1603, and was buried at Wotton May 31), Robert Evelyn succeeded to an estate at Godstone, Surrey; and in the same year (1603), we are informed that a settlement of the manor of Godstone was made, on his marriage with "Susanna, daughter of Gregory Yung, of the county of York, Esq." It is likely that soon after his father's death Robert became involved in debt, and sold the Godstone estate to his brother John, who fixed his residence at Godstone; though the estate was, about 1610, conveyed to Sir William Walter of Wimbledon, by the Evelyn family, as an indemnity for securities which he had entered into for them. In county histories and in family records there is little more told of Robert Evelyn, except that he died before the year 1639.

From the table of descent, annexed, it will be seen that Robert had a large family of seven daughters and three sons; and that his second son, Robert, emigrated to America, the West Indies being a general term for all transatlantic voyages. The male representatives of this branch of the Evelyn family are supposed to be extinct, but it is very probable that there are many English families descended from Robert Evelin, in the female line.

We subjoin a copy of the fragment of a letter, evidently written by Robert Evelin on his departure from England. The letter is addressed to his "mother," that is, to his stepmother Joan, his father's widow. The allusion to his sister and brother Stoughton, shews that the letter must have been written before Nov. 11, 1610, on which day Mrs. Stoughton died. Mrs. Stoughton (born Catharine Evelyn) was Robert's half-sister, and was married to Thomas, son of Lawrence Stoughton, Esq., of Stoughton in Stoke, near Guildford. The letter therefore was written before Nov. 1610, and after the year 1606, when the will of Robert's father was proved. We may assign the year 1609 as the probable date of the letter.

The "brother Richard" of the letter is his half-brother Richard, of Wotton, afterwards father of the author of "Sylva." The "Mr. Comber" mentioned in the letter, was a relative of the family, and probably identical with William Comber, one of the "overseers" of the will of George Evelyn, Robert's father.

It is to be regretted that the original letter is imperfect, and very difficult to decipher. Date and signature are wanting: a few words required to complete the sense have been conjecturally supplied within brackets: the spelling has been modernized. The table of descent will shew the posterity of Robert, so far as can be gathered from the family records. Our authorities for the above facts about Robert Evelyn, or Evelin, as he calls himself, are, first, the records preserved at Wotton House, and secondly, the various notices in Manning and Bray's "History of Surrey," published in 1809.

From the records at Wotton House.—Fragment of a letter (dated probably about 1609) from Robert Evelin (or Evelyn) to his step-mother, Mrs. Joan Evelyn, relict of George Evelyn, of Wotton, Surrey, Esq., who died May 29, 1603 :—

"MOTHER EVELYN,—I commend me most particularly unto you and to my brother Richard, hoping in God of your good health, which I beseech God long to continue to his will and pleasure with much comfort and happiness. I am very sorry that I am morgaged so much, that I am driven to tell you to pay the hundred marks to Mr. Stoughton for me, which you, at my request, did stand bound so kindly for me to him. I am much grieved at my heart for it that my estate is so mean, that at this time I am not able to repay it; but if it be God's pleasure to restore me, I will repay it again to your good liking. I am going to the sea, a long and dangerous vo[yage, with] other men, to make me to be [able] to pay my debts, and to restore my decayed estate again; which, I beseech God of His mercy to grant it, may be [made] prosperous unto me to His honour, and my comfort in this world and in the world to come; and I beseech you, if I do die, that you would be good unto my poor wife and children, which, God knows, I shall leave very poor and very mean, if my friends be not good unto them, for my sins have deserved these punishments and far greater at God's hands, which I humbly beseech God of His mercy to [pardon]. I would have gladly seen you and my brother at this time, but that the captain of the ship made such haste away so suddenly. I am very sorry for the debts of my sister and brother Stoughton, but we must all be contented with the pleasure of Almighty God. [Whenever] it is His pleasure to dispose of us, no doubt they are most happy and blessed, and at rest with God and out of this troublesome world. My wife commends her unto you, and we do [heartily and] most humbly thank you for your love and care of her; and I pray God give her years to shew herself dutiful unto you for it, and thankful, and to her unkle. My mother Yunge, and my brother Morris and his wife, commend them unto you, and I would entreat you commend us unto Mr. Comber and his wife, and Mr. Yunge and his wife; and I would entreat my brother Richard, and Mr. Comber, to do me this kindness, that when [they] go to London, they would sometimes see my wife, and that she may not think that all my friends have forsaken her; and that my brother Richard would do me this kindness, as to give my mother Yunge thank for her [great] care of me and my children, and I shall be very bound to him for it."

In the "History of the County of Kent," in the eastern shore of Maryland, I find the following extract:—

"It now became necessary to extend and establish the civil authority of the Lord Proprietor over the Island (Kent), as a part of the Province of Maryland. Accordinly, on the 30th day of December, 1637, Leonard Calvert, Governor of Maryland, constituted and appointed his 'good friend Captain George Evelyn, of the Isle' commonly called 'Kent,' to be commander of the said Island, and the inhabitants thereof."

This George was in all probability the elder brother of the younger Robert Evelyn, who died in the West Indies.

DESCENDANTS OF ROBERT EVELYN.

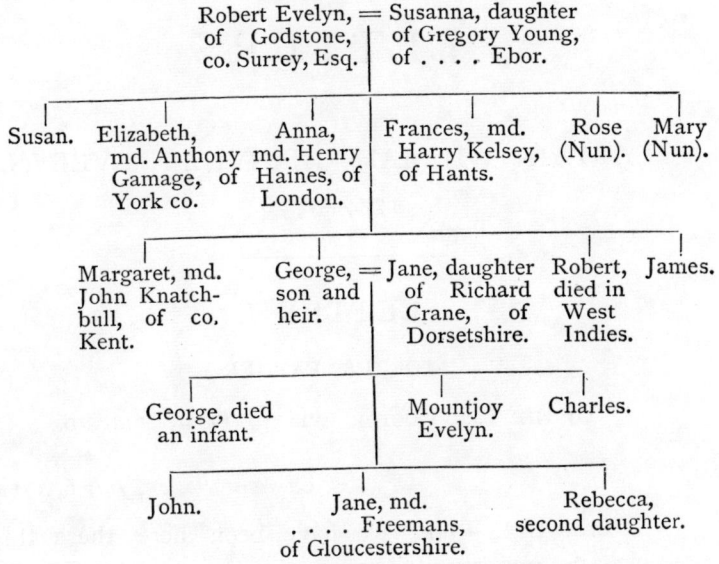

LETTERS

OF

CAPTAIN WILLIAM GLANVILLE EVELYN, 1774—1776.

LETTER I.

(TO HIS FATHER.)

TO THE REV. DOCTOR EVELYN, TRIM, IRELAND.

"*Camp at Boston, July* 6, 1774.

"DEAR SIR,—Tho' we have been here these three weeks, no opportunity has before this time offered of transmitting a letter to Europe. Admiral Montague[a] being now relieved on this station, we avail ourselves of his return to inform our friends of our safe arrival.

---

[a] "Admiral George Montague, as post-captain, April 15, 1773, was employed at the commencement of the American war, in blockading the parts of Salem and Marblehead. After having captured the 'Washington' of 16 guns, the first vessel of war sent to sea by the American States, he covered the embarkation of the army at the evacuation of Boston, where, it is said, he was put in the stocks for walking the streets on a Sunday. By way of retaliation, on the day before the place was abandoned, he invited the mayor and aldermen to dinner, and ordered his boatswain to give them a dozen lashes each. After having assisted at the siege of New York, where his vessel, the 'Fowey,' was stationed, his health being much impaired, he returned to England."—*Georgian Era*, vol. ii. p. 551.

"We sailed from St. Helen's [b] on the 28th of May, and with some fair and some hard-blowing weather, we made this harbour the 10th of June, which we account a good passage. We continued on board our vessels three days, and on the 14th, had the assurance to land, notwithstanding the violent threat denounced against us, and that evening encamped on a small common on the west side of the town (I may say in the town) without any let or molestation. On the day following, the 43rd regiment disembarked and encamped along with us; and just now the 5th and 38th are arrived from Ireland, landed and encamped in the same line, which with a small park of artillery, of six pieces of cannon and two cohorns, make a formidable appearance; we besides expect to be shortly re-inforced, our transports having gone to New York for the 23rd regiment, and the 59th being talked of to come from Halifax; and for a *corps de reserve*, the 64th is in Castle William, a small fortified island in the harbour.

"With this force, we have no apprehensions from the very great numbers in this province, should they ever come to extremities, as they sometimes affect to insinuate; for though upon paper they are the bravest fellows in the world, yet in reality I believe there does not exist so great a set of rascals and poltroons. You who have seen mobs, generous ones compared to these, may have some idea of the wretched situation of those who were known

[b] St. Helen's, a road or bay on the north-east coast of the Isle of Wight, so named from a village in the island. It was a well-known place of rendezvous for the British navy. The roadstead of St. Helen's is the east entrance to the famous roadstead of Spithead, between Portsmouth and Ryde. At St. Helen's the East India fleet used to stop for water and provisions, both in going out and coming in.

or suspected to be friends to the King or government of Great Britain; they are distinguished here by the name of Tories, as the Liberty Boys, the tarring-and-feathering gentlemen, are by the title of Whigs. To the former our arrival has, in a great degree, restored that liberty they have been so long deprived of, even liberty of speech and security to their persons and property, which has for years past been at the mercy of a most villainous mob. General Gage, as Governor of the Province, and Commander-in-chief of the troops, has greater powers than any of his predecessors. He has already dissolved the Council; though they, suspecting his intention, locked out his Secretary, and would not admit him till they had chosen a Committee of Correspondence to settle measures with the other colonies, to force England into a compliance with their terms by means of an association not to import or buy any English goods, not to serve Ireland with flax-seed, nor the West India Islands with provisions or other commodities. Against this Committee the Governor has issued a [firm] and spirited Proclamation, calling it illegal and tr[aitorous,] forbidding all people to sign or offer it to be sign[ed, if they would] avoid the penalties annexed to such aggravated offences; notwithstanding which it has gone on, [and] has been since the Proclamation signed by [many]. But the Tories have taken courage, and made a protest against such unlawful proceedings.

"What all this will end in it is impossible to guess. Great Britain has it in her power now to keep America in the dependence she has a right to insist on; but much is to be feared from the unsteadiness of the English Government, the intrigues of a disaffected faction at home, and the stubbornness and perseverance of the enemies to all Government here; what ever will be the issue, the scourge at present falls upon this part of the province, and most deservedly; for they are a most execrable set of villains.

"I do not see any chance of matters being adjusted; and till that happens we shall probably remain here. I shall from time to time inform you of what is going forward as far as comes to my knowledge, and hope now and then to hear from you. This country is very fine, the climate wholesome, and we all in good health and spirits, and we get plenty of turtle, pine-apples, and Madeira.

"My best love to all at home, and am,
"Dear Sir,
"Your ever affectionate,
"W. G. EVELYN."

———◆———

LETTER II.

To the Honble. Mrs. Leveson Gower (his Cousin), South-street, Grosvenor-square, London.

"*Boston Camp, August the 26th,* 1774.

"MADAM,—As you are now more interested than ever in the affairs of this country, I'm happy to have so good an opportunity as the return of the 'Scarbro',' to give you such accounts of our private concerns here as I hope will be satisfactory to you, and quiet any little fears or uneasiness your mama may be under for the safety or success of her young soldier[c]; I wrote a few days after

---

[c] Alluding to George Evelyn Boscawen, his kinsman, who went out with him, as a young ensign of seventeen, to join his regiment. He

his arrival by a vessel just going to sail, and he also sent a letter by the same ship. Capt. Chadets is now under orders, and only waits for the General's despatches, which are hourly expected; and it would be unpardonable in us not to let you know by him that, since our coming here, we have been in perfect good health and spirits, and seem to agree very well with the new trade of soldiering; we work very hard every morning at the firelock, and have already mounted guard with a command of forty men; we improve very much, and are daily getting the better of those little exceptionable inclinations, which a profession less active would have only contributed to encourage. Believe me, madam, there is no better school in the world to correct any little peculiarity of temper or disposition, and I will venture to stake my credit that, when you next see *the young General*, you shall approve him; this is a name the boys have given him from the gravity of his deportment, and some alterations he has proposed to have made in the management of our affairs; you must know that upon his first coming among us, he discovered that the system we had followed for many years was all wrong, and proceeded to lay down some re-

was the son of the Honble. Edward Boscawen, Admiral of the Blue, R.N., who died in 1761. Young Boscawen was commissioned as Ensign to the 4th foot on May 9, 1774; was promoted to Lieutenant in the 63rd foot on Dec. 1, 1775; to Captain in the 5th Dragoons on Nov. 4, 1777; and sold out Dec. 31, 1782.

He returned to England in 1775, and eventually became third Viscount Falmouth, on the death of his uncle in 1782. He was born May 6, 1758, and died Feb. 8, 1808; and was grandfather of Evelyn, sixth and present Viscount Falmouth, of the county of Cornwall. The Honble. Mrs. Leveson Gower was the sister of George Evelyn Boscawen, and married the Honble. John Leveson Gower, Admiral in the R.N., and brother to Granville, first Marquis of Stafford, who was great-uncle to Colonel E. W. Vernon Harcourt, M.P.

gulations for us, and to set us to rights; but to his great amazement the boys only laughed at his schemes, and called him *Humphrey Bland*[d] and *the young General*, and I am afraid have laughed him out of his plan of reforming the army, for he seems now inclined to go on as other people do.

"I copied my cousin's pleasant letter, for I value the original prodigiously; it is a natural description of a boy who has studied *Bland* during the whole voyage.

"Once more adieu.

"W. G. EVELYN."

LETTER III.

TO THE HONBLE. MRS. LEVESON GOWER, SOUTH-STREET, GROSVENOR-SQUARE, LONDON.

"*Camp at Boston, Oct.* 31, 1774.

"DEAR MADAM,—The receipt of your last letter filled me with the utmost surprise and concern; that change of constitution, from great robustness to extreme delicacy, I always imagined had proceeded from the inactive kind of life Mr. Boscawen[e] had led; but never in the least suspected it to be the consequence of any disorder or want

[d] A manual for young soldiers, written by Humphrey Bland, called "Military Discipline," published in London in 1727. The ninth edition of this book was published in 1762.

I have found mention of an Honble. Colonel Humphrey Bland, as having commanded a regiment of foot, no doubt the 36th.

[e] Alluding to the death of the son of the Honble. Mrs. Boscawen, which is thus mentioned in the "Gentleman's Magazine," under date of July 17, 1774 :—

"At the German Spa, Hugh Boscawen, Esq., son of the late Admiral, nephew to Lord Falmouth, brother-in-law to the Duke of Beaufort, and member for Truro in Cornwall."

of health. My immediate anxiety and concern are employed for the situation of your most excellent and unparalleled mother; ill calculated from too much sensibility to bear such repeated strokes, that revive the remembrance of misfortunes in some degree softened by length of time, but now renewed with unproved affliction.

"As one wishes to draw consolation from the most distant source, I should hope her sufferings on this occasion were much alleviated by her having been for several years accustomed to live without him, and to consider him in a great degree as separated from her; we have to be thankful that the scene of this misfortune was at a distance, whereby many additional circumstances of pain were avoided.

"I observed your command, and was the first to communicate it to George, but with a great deal of precaution, and not till I had first prepared him. I was very much pleased with his manner of receiving it, which was full of sensibility, affection, and manly concern, as he has since conducted himself with the greatest propriety. If I could not speak of him in such a manner as I think would give you satisfaction, I should say no more than that he was in good health, for it is a matter in which I would not deceive you: but I have the greatest reason to believe he will merit the approbation of his friends, and do honour to his family. He has exceeding good principles, and an amazing fund of understanding, both of which will be of the greatest use to us in counteracting some little propensities, which I hope are more the effect of too much liberty at Winchester[f] than of natural dis-

---

[f] Extract from a letter from Mrs. Delany to Bernard Granville, Esq., Aug. 1, 1774:—" Her (Mrs. Boscawen) youngest (and *now only*) son

position; you will conceive I allude to his love of indolence and luxury. To these we shall oppose the powerful force of habit; be that my care.

"I already see its effect, and do assure you he is not only exceedingly improved in his manner, but in his air and person. I hope your Mama has no thoughts of his going home; whatever turn affairs may take, it is his interest to remain here some time longer, after which it would not be improper to look out for a Lieutenancy for him in some regiment lately come home, and in England; but by no means ever think of putting him into the Guards, or suffering him to be about London.

"We still remain in our Camp on the Common; but expect in a fortnight or three weeks time to get into

had gone through Winchester School with great credit, and she had promised herself great satisfaction in his making a figure as a man of learning in some profession, and was preparing him for the University, when a frenzy of going into the army seized him, and he would listen to no other occupation. Mrs. Boscawen thought it to no purpose to thwart an inclination that had taken such root, consented, and he sailed with the regiment he is in for America above a month ago; so one may say she is deprived of all her sons."—*From the Autobiography and Correspondence of Mary Granville (Mrs. Delany),* 1862.

From the Honble. Mrs. Boscawen to Mrs. Delany, May 13, 1774:—
"Your cousin Mrs. Leveson is in perfect health, and in the evening Mr. George reads to us Lord Chesterfield's letters, (note, Lord C. died in 1773; his Letters were published in 1774), of which, I think just as you do, and therefore very right, I doubt not. My son George is clear in his choice of arms, and I have at his desire paid £400 for an ensigncy in the 4th Foot, or King's Own Regiment lately sailed for America, where my young soldier purposes to join them in the course of this summer, full as well stored with Greek and Latin as my Lord Chesterfield. Oh! my dear boy, I did not intend him for this business; but I submit, and hope time and his good behaviour will reconcile me to it better than I now am, or can be as yet."

F

barracks. I have taken a house for George and myself, and we hope to pass the winter comfortably; it is very lucky for us that at this season we have the finest weather in the whole year, for the good people of this place have done everything in their power to prevent our getting quarters, and to distress us by forbidding all labourers and artificers to work for us; by hindering the merchants to supply us with blankets, tools, or materials of any kind; by burning the straw provided in the country for the troops, and threatening to stop all provisions coming to the market; but money (for which these holy men would sell the Kingdom of Heaven) defeats their charitable intentions, and we happen to have artificers enough among our men, with the help of ship-carpenters and others sent us from New York and Halifax, to fit up our distilleries and warehouses without their assistance.

"A reinforcement of troops is just arrived, Captain Wallis, in the 'Rose' man-of-war, has brought two companies of the 65th regiment from Newfoundland; Mr. Bourmaster is just come in with his transports from New York, bringing General Haldimand [g] with the 47th regiment, and part of the 18th. With them is also my old friend Colonel Prescott [h], two of the Quebec fleet with the 10th and 52nd regiments are in the harbour, and the others expected hourly. What all this preparation will end in, you, who have an opportunity of knowing how far the people at home are disposed, may give some guess; but were we to judge from the spirit and proceedings of the people here, we should conclude that a civil war must inevitably

---

[g] Governor-General of Canada in 1777.
[h] For an account of Colonel Prescott (afterwards Brigadier-General), see Appendix.

happen in the course of a few months, or that Great Britain must for ever give up America.

"This whole country is just now in a state of actual open rebellion; there is not a man from sixteen to sixty, nay, to a hundred years old, who is not armed and obliged to attend at stated times to train; there is no act of treason or rebellion which they have not committed, except that of actually attacking the troops, from which they are restrained only by a dread of the consequences; they have less to fear from assassination, and there are at this moment two of their agents in the jail of Boston, one for attempting the lives of Colonel Cleveland [i] of the Artillery and Captain Montresor [k] of the Engineers, the other for surprising a soldier and wounding him with a sword. The most respectable gentlemen, and those of the greatest property in the country, in general disavow and protest against the violent proceedings of the faction, for which they are compelled to fly from their houses and families, and shelter themselves under the protection of the troops.

[i] For an account of Colonel Cleveland, see Appendix.

[k] In 1777, Capt. John Montresor was an aide to Sir William Howe; in 1778, was made Chief Engineer of North America, and he was no doubt a relation of Colonel John Montresor, called the "Chief Engineer in America," who wrote "a journal of the expedition across Maine to Quebec in 1775," which was published in 1831, with a number of General Arnold's letters included in it, by the Maine Historical Society. Capt. Montresor was present at (in May, 1778), and acted as one of the managers of, the celebrated ball called the "Meschianza," which was given in Philadelphia, by the British officers, to Sir William Howe, on the eve of his departure for England. Captain Montresor, the engineer, it is stated, had charge of the fireworks and the ballroom decorations. Watson the Annalist states "that there were no ladies of British officers present at the entertainment, except Miss Auchmuty, the new bride of Captain Montresor." The Le Tresors, or Montresors, were an old Huguenot family settled in England, several of whom rose to distinction in the British army.

Should any of these gentlemen venture home, the alarm is immediately spread, his house surrounded by hundreds of armed men; and should he fall into their hands, he is very fortunate if he gets off for signing, swearing, and publishing whatsoever it shall please them in their fury to dictate.

"Mr. Ingersoll[1], who is so kind as to take charge of this letter, is one of those who have experienced their treatment; if you should see him, and have any curiosity to enquire about the state of this country, he can give you a very full and circumstantial [account]. I can only say, from the short acquaintance I have with the holy men of Massachusetts, I firmly believe that so execrable a set of sanctified villains never before disgraced the human species.

"Before this can arrive, the time will be past on which you should receive some money from my father and me. I believe you understand he has taken upon him to pay forty guineas yearly, which, with the enclosed bill upon our agents for nineteen pounds, makes the sum of 61 pounds, one year's interest for £900 at 5 per cent., and of £400 at 4 per cent. I have also written to him by this opportunity to remind him that it is become due, and I am very happy to have so good a one, as the common conveyance by post is no longer safe. As we have reason to believe that more troops and men-of-war will be sent out in the spring, there are a few things which George would be very glad to receive by them; such as a few pairs of ribbed thread and silk stockings, a hat or two, and a couple of silver table-spoons, but nothing would be

---

[1] Probably Jared Ingersoll, the stamp-master, who was burned in effigy in 1765.

more acceptable than a cask of porter, as our only liquor for the table here is a stuff they call spruce beer. I mentioned my old tutor, Colonel Prescott[m], having arrived here: he is come a volunteer to offer his services, and I hope will be allowed to remain among us; he is the man to whom I am indebted for my military education; he has begun already to assist me with his good counsel and advice, which [no one] is more capable of giving, both from his abilities and experience; [he begs] me to present his respectful compliments to your Mama, [and assu]re her that nothing will give him greater pleasure than to [have] opportunities of being in any way serviceable to her son George, for which I have already thanked him in her name.

"In short, Madam, I hope you will be perfectly easy on his account. He is in a very good line, and will yet turn out a clever fellow. I can only say for myself, that the most unremitted care and attention on my part will but poorly express with how much gratitude and affection

"I am, dear Madam,

"Your ever obliged and obedient servant,

"W. G. EVELYN."

[m] For an account of Colonel, afterwards Brigadier-General Prescott, see Appendix.

LETTER IV.

To the Rev. Doctor Evelyn (his Father), Trim, Ireland.

"*Boston Camp, October* 31*st,* 1774.

"My dear Sir,—It happens so seldom that we have the opportunity of a King's ship going from hence, that we are glad to lay hold of every one that offers to let our friends hear from us; they must be a good deal alarmed for us indeed, if ever they see the bold and desperate resolves of every village in New England, and must conclude that two or three thousand poor fellows of us must have long since been devoured by men of their mighty stomachs; but here we still are in our peaceful camp, and in the same situation as when I last wrote to you; nothing of any consequence has happened, but great preparations for hostilities making on both sides. We, on our part, have fortified the only entrance to the town by land, and thrown up a very extensive work in front of it. We have got General Haldimand, with the 47th Regiment and part of the 18th, from New York, with more artillery and military stores; two other Regiments, the 10th and 52nd, are coming in from Quebec, part of them already in the harbour; and we have a man-of-war, and two companies of the 65th from Newfoundland.

"The good people of these Provinces are getting ready as fast as they can; they are all provided with arms and ammunition, and every man who is able to use them is obliged to repair at stated times to the place of exercise in order to train; in short, the frenzy with which the people are seized is now got to such a pitch, that it can go but little farther, and they must either soon, very soon, break out into civil war, or take that turn which the people of England did at the time of the Restoration, and wreak their vengeance on those who have seduced and misled them. I believe never was so much mercy extended to any nation on the face of the earth: they are now in an absolute, open, avowed state of rebellion, and have committed every act of treason which can be devised, but that of openly attacking the troops, which they publicly declare their resolution of doing as soon as they are prepared, and the season will allow them, and they feel bold.

"The people of England, in the time of Charles the First, behaved with decency and moderation compared with these. The 'North Briton,' 'Whisperer,' 'Parliamentary Spy,' 'Junius,' &c., are dutiful and respectful addresses compared to the publications here; never before did I see treason and rebellion naked and undisguised; it is the only occasion upon which they lay aside hypocrisy. We expected to have been in barracks by this time, but the sons of liberty have done every thing in their power to prevent our accommodation. As it was found difficult to furnish quarters for so many men, it was resolved (to avoid extremities) to build barracks on the Common, where we are encamped; for some regiments timber was provided, and the frames pretty well advanced, when they thought proper to issue their orders to the carpenters to desist from working for the troops, upon pain of their displeasure. And one man who paid no attention to their order, was waylaid, seized by the mob, and carried off, and narrowly escaped hanging. However, the Government have procured distilleries and vacant warehouses sufficient to hold all the regiments, and our own artificers, with those of the men-of-war, and about 150 from New York and Halifax, are now at work upon them, and we hope to get into them in ten days or a fortnight. They have also forbid all merchants from furnishing their enemies with blankets, tools, or materials of any kind, [and have] endeavoured to hinder our getting bricks to build chimneys in our barracks, and threatened to prohibit all provisions being brought to market; but the force of English gold no Yankey can withstand, were it offered to purchase his salvation. I can give you no description of the 'holy men of Massachusetts,' by which you can form a just idea of what they are. There are no instances in history to compare them by; the Jews at the time of the siege of Jerusalem seem to come [near them], but are injured and disgraced by the comparison.

"By the time you receive this, I believe Mrs. Boscawen will look to hear from you and me on the subject of money; depending on your punctuality in remitting the part you were pleased to take upon yourself, I have sent by this opportunity a bill upon our agent for the remainder, which will discharge the year's interest due last August or September; and I have informed Mrs. Boscawen that she will receive forty guineas from you. Not knowing what hour the 'St. Lawrence' will sail, I can only tell you that Boscawen is grown a stout fellow, and is much improved. We are both very well, and have taken a house for the winter. I beg my best love to all my friends; I should be glad to hear something of them when you have a spare half-hour.

"I am, dear Sir,
"Your ever affectionate,
"W. G. EVELYN."

LETTER V.

To the Honble. Mrs. Leveson Gower, South-street, Grosvenor-square.

"*Boston, December 6th,* 1774.

"Madam,—We embrace with great pleasure every safe opportunity that offers to inform you that we continue to go on as well and as successfully as we could expect or desire. Since our last packets, which went by the 'St. Lawrence' schooner, we have exchanged our houses of canvas for others of wood, which are rather a better defence against the severity of the weather that we are told we may expect, for as yet we know very little of it, having at present as fine and as delightful a season as you have in England in the month of April. Mr. Champagné[n], George and I, live together, and take it in turn week about to be purveyors, and are, I assure you, no despicable housekeepers. We have laid in a tolerable

---

[n] His friend Mr. Champagné, was left one of Capt. Evelyn's executors, and is no doubt the Lieutenant Champagné who was wounded on the British side at the battle of Germantown, in Oct. 1777. Capt. Evelyn's will was probably confided to his friend Lieut. Champagné, as Capt. Balfour, another executor, was in England. The family of Champagné had been settled in Ireland since the revocation of the Edict of Nantes. The progenitor of the family was Josias de Robillard, Seigneur de Champagné. On arriving in Ireland he assumed the name of Champagné. They were related, as well as the Balfours of Townley Hall, Ireland, to the family of the Earls of Enniskillen.

Lieut. Champagné re-appears at the south under Lord Cornwallis, and with Gen. Tarleton, as Capt. Champagné, in an unsuccessful attempt to capture Thomas Jefferson, and the members of the North Caroline legislature, at Charlottesville, in June, 1781.

good stock of Port and Madeira, and hope to spend the winter as well as our neighbours. Housekeeping at first setting out, is, as you know, always attended with some little extraordinary expense, in consequence of which we have drawn another small bill in favour of the same Mr. Dumaresq' for about twelve pounds, which by-the-bye is scarcely sufficient; but the demand for money here is so great, and all trade with England being at a stand, that it is almost impossible to get cash for a small bill, even by paying from two and a-half to five per cent. exchange. . . . . . . If you should be in town, this letter will be delivered to you by Colonel Prescott, who has obtained leave to go home, and has most obligingly desired to be charged with our letters, that he may have an opportunity of seeing your Mama, and giving her pleasing and satisfactory accounts of her son.

"In my last, I mentioned his civility upon his arrival here, for which I am sure he will have your thanks. I was in hopes he would have been appointed to some command here; and I regret very much that he leaves us at this time, not only on account of my losing a friend, whose good offices I might have expected, but because I know his abilities as an officer to be of the first class, and such as we shall probably have occasion for very soon.

"I need not say anything on the present state of this country, for that subject I refer you to the bearer; but we are all in high spirits at the speedy return of the 'Scarbro',' and of this re-inforcement of men-of-war. We hope they are an earnest of the spirited resolutions of the people at home, no longer to suffer the treason and rebellion of these villains to go unpunished. Never did any nation so much deserve to be made an example of to future ages, and never were any set of men more anxious [than we] to be employed on so laudable a work. We only fear they will avail themselves of the clemency and generosity of the English, and by some abject submission evade the chastisement due to unexampled villainy, and which we are so impatiently waiting to inflict.

"I am very glad to observe that your Mama has never expressed any desire of having George home again: indeed, at present it would not only be imprudent, but impracticable, as nobody whose regiment is here is suffered to go home. I had a proposal some time ago, from a gentleman in the Governor's family, to exchange into Sir Adolphus Oughton's regiment, lately gone home; but whatever desire I might have to be in England, or to serve under a Colonel who I should hope would conceive no unjust or ill-grounded prejudices against me, circumstanced as matters are at present, I thought it my duty to decline it.

"The ship which carries our letters is one of our transports, sent home, as 'tis said, for the purpose of bringing out necessaries for the use of the troops, as there is no doubt but this non-importation scheme will create a scarcity, and raise the price of many articles. It would not therefore be amiss, if Mr. Steer would take the trouble of walking to one Mr. Busshers, in Bedford-street, Covent Garden (who supplies our regiment with cloth of all sorts), and would order him to pack up scarlet and white, and some blue cloth sufficient for two suits, with serge, &c., the proper quantity of regimental buttons, and two epaulettes, directed for Ensign Boscawen of the King's Own Regiment, to be sent on board the 'Charming Nancy,' Captain Deverson. Mr. Steer might in his return call upon Mr. Oliphant, and order a couple of plain hats, with silver buttons and loops for ditto; and might moreover be very useful in providing any other things which you might think acceptable to a poor fellow at a great distance.

"He acquainted me with your Mama's very kind offer of settling my business this year with Mr. Dymoke. I am already too much indebted to her generosity, and ashamed to have been ever a perpetual tax upon her. I hope she is not offended at my declining to accept it; it did not put me to the smallest inconvenience. I sent a bill upon our agents for nineteen pounds by the 'St. Lawrence,' and wrote at the same time to my father to remit the rest, as he promised he would when we parted. 'Tis all I trouble him for, and I should be glad to find he is more punctual in that than in writing to me, for I have not had one line from him since I came to America.

"I find it would have been a lucky circumstance, for me at least a pleasant one, had I brought out any letters of recommendation to the General, Mrs. Gage, Lord Percy[o], or any of the great folks here. I do not mean by this that you should put yourself to the trouble of procuring any, as I know your readiness to interest yourself for me upon all occasions. I only mean, that if you should meet with any among your acquaintance who have any correspondence with the great people, and who would not think it a mighty obligation to mention one's name, it is sometimes of use to be made known to them.

"I hope Mr. Leveson and his son[p] continue in good health. We are a good deal surprised to hear of his recovery, as we had never heard he had been ill.

[o] For Lord Percy, see Appendix.
[p] John Leveson, the eldest son of Admiral the Honble. John Leveson (Gower).

"I beg my best respects to him, my duty to your Mama, and that you will believe me to be,

"Madam,

"Your most sincerely obliged and obedient servant,

"W. G. EVELYN."

LETTER VI.

TO THE REVEREND DOCTOR EVELYN (HIS FATHER), TRIM, IRELAND.

"*Boston, Feb. 18th*, 1775.

"MY DEAR SIR,—About the 10th of this month, I received your letter (the only one I have got from you) dated the 2nd of November, though it was not opened, as mine to you had been, yet it did not fall short of it in expense, as every letter we receive by the New York Packet costs us threepence for every pennyweight; for which reason I wish our friends would endeavour to write to us by vessels bound to Salem or Marble Head, or try to have their letters sent in General Gage's bag, as Mr. Butler sends his to his son, and saves him by that means fifteen or twenty shillings a-month. If you would be kind enough to enclose any letter for me to him, I am sure he would be so obliging as to send it to the Secretary of State's office in England, and I should receive it with the General's despatches.

"I was a good deal alarmed at the account you gave me of the violent fit which attacked you; but your being again so well recovered, makes me hope that nothing remains of it but the apprehension.

"That lies innumerable should be circulated in your papers with regard to what is passing here is no way strange, when in this very town, where we are upon the spot, the most false, impudent, and incredible relations are every day published concerning us; but the fact is, the authors know them to be false, and that not a person in this town (of about twenty thousand inhabitants) believes a word of them; but they are calculated for the poor deluded wretches in the country, who are all politicians, and swallow everything they see in those seditious papers (and none other are they allowed to read) with a credulity not equalled even in old England; and by this means is the spirit of faction kept alive, and the schemes of a few enterprising, ambitious demagogues made to pass upon the people for their own act and deed. I said *of a few;* a great many doubtless appear to be concerned in carrying on the business; but would you believe it, that this immense continent from New England to Georgia is moved and directed by one man[q]! a man of ordinary birth and desperate fortune, who by his abilities and talent for factious intrigue, has made himself of some consequence, whose political existence depends upon the continuance of the present dispute, and who must sink into insignificancy and beggary the moment it ceases.

"People in general are inclined to attribute the ferment that at present subsists in this country to a settled plan

---

[q] "Samuel Adams," wrote Galloway, "though by no means remarkable for brilliant abilities, is equal to most men in popular intrigue, and the management of a faction. He eats little, drinks little, sleeps little, and thinks much, and is most decisive and indefatigable in the pursuit of his objects. He was the man who, by his superior application, managed at once the faction in Congress at Philadelphia, and the factions in New England."

and system, formed and prosecuted for some years past by a few ambitious, enterprising spirits; but in my opinion the true causes of it are to be found in the nature of mankind; and [I think] that it proceeds from a new nation, feeling itself wealthy, populous, and strong; and [that they] being impatient of restraint, are struggling to throw off that dependency which is so irksome to them. The other seems to me to be only the consequence; such a time being most apt for men of abilities, but desperate fortunes, to set themselves forward to practise upon the passions of the people, foment that spirit of opposition to all law and government, and to urge them on to sedition, treason, and rebellion, in hopes of profiting by the general distraction.

"This is the case of our great patriot and leader, Sam Adams[r]. Hancock[s], and those others whose names you

---

[r] The Venerable John Adams, in a short autobiography written at Quincy, Dec. 30, 1815, says:—"The late Governor, Samuel Adams, was not my brother. He was no nearer relation to me than a second cousin: we had the same great-grandfather. John, was my father; Joseph, junior, was my grandfather; the oldest son of Joseph Adams, senior, my great-grandfather. Governor Adams was the son of Samuel Adams of Boston; the grandson of John Adams of Boston; and the great-grandson of Joseph Adams, senior, of this parish, now called Quincy, who was the common ancestor of us both."

[s] From the "New York Journal." Extract from a letter dated Boston, March 22, 1775:—"On the 17th, in the evening, Col. Hancock's elegant seat, situate near the common, was attacked by a number of officers, who with their swords cut and hacked the fence before his house in a most scandalous manner, and behaved very abusively, by breaking people's windows, and almost insulting every person they met." "On the evening of the 18th, a number of officers (heated with liquor as is said) with drawn swords ran through the streets, like what they really were, madmen, cutting every one they met. The stage coach, just arrived from Providence, passing by, they attacked it, broke the glass, and abused the passengers; the driver being

hear, are but his mere tools; though many of them are men of no mean abilities. Hancock is a poor contemptible fool, led about by Adams, and has spent a fortune of thirty thousand pounds upon that infamous crew; has sacrificed all he was worth in the world to the vanity of being admitted among them, and is now nearly reduced to a state of beggary. The steps by which the *sons of liberty* have proceeded, and the strides with which they are now hasting to rebellion and civil war, are set forth in a very masterly manner by a writer (on our side), under the signature of Massachusettensis [t]; which papers,

a smart fellow, jumped off his seat, caught one of them (Captain G.), and some blows passed, when the officer retired, not much to his credit." "On the 19th, Colonel Hancock was again much insulted by a number of inferior officers and privates, who entered his enclosures, and refused to retire, after his requesting them so to do, telling him that his house, stables, &c., would soon be theirs, and they would do as they pleased. However, on his application to the General, he immediately sent one of his aides-de-camp to the officer of the guard at the bottom of the common, to seize any officer or private who should molest Colonel Hancock, or any inhabitant in their lawful calling."

[t] This is the full title of this, now, rare little work :—
"*Massachusettensis;* or, A Series of Letters containing a faithful state of many important and striking facts, which laid the foundation of the present troubles in the Province of the Massachusetts bay, interspersed with animadversions and reflections originally addressed to the People of the Province, and worthy the consideration of the True Patriots of this Country. By a person of honour upon the spot.—

"'Falsus honor juvat et mendax infamia terret
Quem nisi mendosum et mendacem? Vir bonus est quis?
Qui consulta patrum, qui leges juraque servat.'
Horace, Ep. xvi."

Which may be thus rendered into English :—
"Whom does false honour please, or lying slander terrify, except the vicious and the false? Who is a good man? He who observes the decrees of the Senate, the laws and rules of justice."

Capt. W. G. Evelyn.

as far as they have been hitherto published, I have enclosed to Mr. Butler at the Castle, directed for you; they will give you a better idea of the nature of this important contest than any on the other side, which are composed of sedition, treason, misrepresentation, and falsehood, framed by villains of the first water, and greedily swallowed with the credulity of ignorance, and the malignant zeal of inveterate fanatics.

"It is but very lately that a Tory writer dare appear, or that a Printer could be prevailed on to publish any thing on the side of Government; and nothing now protects them, but the presence of the troops in Boston. Those who have remained in the country, whose circumstances and situation would not admit of their leaving their families, are hourly in danger. Some are prisoners in their own houses; a mob constantly mounting guard about them, lest they should escape; and others have been treated with the utmost barbarity. Words cannot give you an idea of the nature of the lower class of people in this province: they are utterly devoid of every sentiment of truth or common honesty: they are proscribed throughout the whole Continent, and possess no other

---

"The third edition, Boston printed; London, reprinted for J. Matthews, No. 18 in the Strand, MDCCLXXVI." There is a preface of eight pages, and pp. 118. In all sixteen letters. The first dated Dec. 12, 1774; the last, April 3, 1775.

Until recent years, the authorship of these letters was ascribed to Jonathan Sewell, who was Attorney-General of Massachusetts in 1767. Now, however, it is believed they were written by Daniel Leonard, a native of Norton, Massachusetts, afterwards Chief-Justice of Bermuda. He was opposed to American independence, and is said to have written "Massachusettensis" in opposition to some patriotic pamphlets issued by John Adams, under the signature of Novanglus.

human qualities but such as are the shame and reproach of humanity.

"As the event of this very important question depends upon the determination of the people of Great Britain, and as they have such unhappy divisions, and so many dangerous enemies to their country among themselves, it is impossible to form any conjecture about it. We who know our own powers, and the helpless situation of the people, consider it as the most fortunate opportunity for Great Britain to establish her superiority over this country; even to reduce it to that state of subjection, which the right of conquest may now give her the fairest title to; at least, to keep it in that state of dependency which they are now avowedly attempting to free themselves from, and which, had they waited for another century, they would probably achieve. Though the point at present in view is, to be independent of Great Britain, and to set up for themselves, yet I do not believe the most sanguine of them have any expectation of accomplishing it at this time; but they hope to make some approaches, and to gain something towards it. In this struggle their great dependence is upon the tenderness and clemency of the English, who they imagine will consider them under infatuation, and will give up some points to them out of humanity, rather than push matters to extremity; and indeed, they may with reason think so, for under no other Government on the face of the earth would they have been suffered to perpetrate so many horrid villainies, as they have done, without being declared in a state of rebellion, and having fire and sword let loose among them. From the accounts given by the faction, people would imagine that the colonies were unanimous to a man in their opposition to Government, but the contrary is the

Capt. W. G. Evelyn. 51

fact; there is a very large party in our favour, and thousands inclined to our side, who dare not openly declare themselves, from an apprehension that Government may leave them in the lurch; this you may depend upon as a certain truth, that those gentlemen who have declared on our side are men of the best property in this country, and those who before these troubles were in the highest esteem, and most respected among the common people.

"The hour is now very nigh in which this affair will be brought to a crisis. The resolutions we expect are by this time upon the water, which are to determine the fate of Great Britain and America. We have great confidence in the spirit and pride of our countrymen, that they will not tamely suffer such insolence and disobedience from a set of upstart vagabonds, the dregs and scorn of the human species; and that we shall shortly receive such orders as will authorize us to scourge the rebellion with rods of iron. Under this hope have we been hitherto restrained, and with an unparalleled degree of patience and discipline have we submitted to insults and indignities[u], from villains who are hired to provoke us to something that may be termed an outrage, and turned to our dis-

---

[u] From "New York Journal." Extract from a letter dated Boston, March 22, 1775:—"Since the army has found that the season is past for nature's forming a bridge from hence, they became abusive and insulting. They are now finishing their fortifications on the rocks, by picketing on each side. The 16th inst. (being recommended by the Provincial Congress to be observed as a day of fasting and prayer), on the morning of this day, the Society at the west end of Boston was greatly disturbed by a party of officers and soldiers of the 4th, or King's Own Regiment. When the people were assembling, they brought two markee (*sic*) tents, and pitched them within ten yards of the meeting-house; then sent for three drums, and three fifes, and kept them beating and playing till service was over."

advantage; but these are all treasured up in our memories against that hour in which we shall "cry havock, and let slip the dogs of war." Excuse my indignation, I cannot speak with patience of this generation of vipers. If any troops should be ordered from Ireland with officers of distinction, I should beg your interest to procure me some recommendations.

"The value of recommendations is not to be told. I have the honour of being pretty well known to General Gage, and Lord Percy, who are both very civil to me; and I have lately had a favourable introduction to their notice from a little *jeu d'esprit* that amused them in one of the papers, and which they suspect me of having had a hand in.

"You must not believe implicitly the reports that are spread of the deaths and desertions among the troops; there have been some, and some regiments have been more unlucky than others; but it is very trifling, when you consider that no pains or expenses have been spared to seduce our men. Our regiment, nevertheless, has not lost more than we usually have done in the same length of time in Great Britain. Boscawen, Champagné[x], and I, keep house together. The weather is delightful[y] beyond description, and we are in perfect good health and spirits.

"Wishing the same to all friends at home,
"I am, dear Sir,
"Your ever affectionate,
"W. G. E."

[x] Mr. Champagné, one of his friends.
[y] "The winter (of 1775), at Boston, was the mildest ever known." —(*Bancroft.*)

LETTER VII.

To the Reverend Doctor Evelyn (his Father), Trim,
Ireland.

"*Boston, April* 23*rd*, 1775.

"My dear Sir,—It is impossible but you must hear an account, and probably a most exaggerated one, of the little fracas that happened here a few days ago, between us and the Yankey scoundrels. Our bickerings and heart-burnings, as might naturally be expected, came at length to blows, and both sides have lost some men. Were you not to hear from me on the occasion, you might imagine I was hurt; at least, you expect from me some account of the affair. The rebels, you know, have of a long time been making preparations as if to frighten us, though we always imagined they were too great cowards ever to presume to do it; but though they are the most absolute cowards on the face of the earth, yet they are just now worked up to such a degree of enthusiasm and madness, that they are easily persuaded the Lord is to assist them in whatever they undertake, and that they must be invincible.

"On the night of the 18th instant, the Grenadiers and Light Infantry of our little army, making near 700 men, embarked privately, and crossed above the common ferry here, in order to go to a town about twenty miles off, to destroy some cannon, provisions, &c., that had been collected there; the country having been alarmed by the appearance of troops in the night, they assembled from every quarter; and within about five miles of the place (Concord), our men found themselves opposed by a body of men in arms, whose design appeared to be to stop their progress. This they were soon convinced of, by receiving a scattering shot or two from them, upon which a few of our people fired, and killed seven or eight minute men; and so passed on to Concord, where they destroyed some iron guns, gun-carriage wheels, and about 100 casks of flour.

"On their return to Boston, they were attacked from the woods and houses on each side of the road, and an incessant fire kept up on both sides for several hours; they still retiring through the wood whenever our people advanced upon them. About eight in the evening (the 19th) our brigade, consisting of the 4th, 23rd, 47th regiments, and the Marines, with the six pounders, marched to meet them, little suspecting what was going on; about 3 o'clock we came up with them, and began immediately; we observed on our march as we went, that the houses along the road were all shut up as if deserted, though we afterwards found these houses were full of men, and only forsaken by the women and children; having executed our orders, and being on our return to Boston, we were attacked on all sides, from woods, and orchards, and stone walls, and from every house on the road side (and this country is a continued village), so that for fourteen miles we were attacking fresh posts, and under one incessant fire. We sent out large flanking parties, who soon scoured the woods and stone walls; and whenever we were fired on from houses or barns, our men dashed in, and let very few of those they could find escape.

"The loss of the rebels cannot be ascertained, but we have reason to think several hundreds were killed. Our regiment had four or five men killed, and about twenty-four wounded. Of the whole, about seventy killed, and 150 wounded; among which last were several officers. Considering the circumstances, we should have thought our loss inconsiderable, were it not for the death of one, the most amiable and worthy man in the world. You will be grieved to hear that my poor dear friend, Joe Knight, received a ball through the body, of which he died next day, [to] our unspeakable grief, and the general loss of the whole army. Poor little Gould[z] received a wound a little above his heel, and going home before the division, was intercepted, and is detained among them; but we hear that they do not use him ill, and that he is attended by a surgeon. Boscawen and I escaped unhurt. I wish they would purchase a Lieutenancy for him at home, for I am very uneasy lest anything befall him while he is with me. The country is all in arms, and we are absolutely invested with many thousand men, some of them so daring, as to come very near our outposts on the only entrance into town by the land. They have cut off all supplies of provisions from the country; but we feel no want, having many months' allowance in the harbour. We expect every day the three Generals[a], and a strong re-inforcement of troops from Great Britain and Ireland. I wish they were arrived.

"I shall not fail to write by the first opportunity; in the meantime, my love to all at home, and believe me,

"Dear Sir,

"Your most affectionate,

"W. G. EVELYN."

[z] For "little Gould," see Appendix.
[a] On May 25, 1775, Generals Howe, Clinton, and Burgoyne arrived with reinforcements. Bancroft mentions that they brought their angling-rods with them.

English account of the Battles of Lexington and Concord, taken from " The Historical Record of the 52nd Regiment."

"IN the spring of 1775, General Gage having been informed that the Americans were collecting military stores at Concord, about eighteen miles from Boston, the flank companies of the 52nd, and of several corps, were ordered to proceed on an expedition to destroy the stores, under the command of Lieut.-Colonel Francis Smith, of the 10th Foot; and Major John Pitcairn, of the Marines. The troops embarked in boats at 10 o'clock in the night of the 18th of April, proceeded to the entrance of the Cambridge river; and having landed at Phipp's farm, advanced upon Concord. In the meantime the Americans, by the ringing of bells and the firing of guns, had alarmed the whole neighbourhood. About four o'clock in the morning of the 19th of April, the light company of the 10th being in advance, approached the village of Lexington, where a body of American militia was forming. They were ordered to lay down their arms; but taking shelter behind a stone wall, several of them fired at the King's troops. A volley from the latter laid ten of the militia dead upon the spot, wounded several, and dispersed the rest. This was the first blood drawn in the American war. After this skirmish the troops continued their march to Concord; and as soon as the object of the expedition was accomplished, namely, the destruction of the military stores, they commenced their march upon Boston, under a heavy fire, which was continued by the Americans until the arrival of the force at Lexington, about five miles distant.

"Skirmish succeeded skirmish, until the soldiers were exhausted, and had expended nearly all their ammunition. Fortunately a reinforcement, consisting of a brigade of infantry and two guns, under the command of Colonel Earl Percy, came to their assistance at this place. His Lordship formed his men into a square, with the exhausted flank companies in the centre; and after a short halt, continued the retreat to Charlestown, whence he crossed the river by ferry to Boston, having lost several men from the incessant fire which the Americans kept up from behind walls, trees, and over coverts on both sides of the road.

"The loss of the 52nd was confined to three rank and file killed, two wounded, and one sergeant missing."

In the MS. Diary of Brigadier-General Jedidiah Preble, of Falmouth, under date Wednesday, August 9, 1775, occurs the following entry:—

"Overcast. This morning I met a man that deserted from the regulars this day fortnight; as sensible, intelligent a fellow as I ever met with—he was at Lexington fight. He says he came out with Lord Percy, and that he asked a young fellow of his acquaintance who fired the first. The soldiers, when they came where the Provincials were, one of them flashed his piece, on which a regular officer fired, and swung his gun over his head, and then there was a general fire. They had seventy-five killed and missing, 233 wounded."—*From Historical Magazine (N. Y.),* vol. iii. p. 153, year 1859.

LETTER VIII.

To the Honble. Mrs. Leveson Gower, South-street, Grosvenor-square, London.

"*Camp at Boston, June 6th*, 1775.

"Dear Madam,—Though I have already sent one letter directed for you on board the 'Cerberus,' yet I cannot help adding a little more, to announce the safe arrival of the ordnance ship which brought me your letter, with a particular account of my father's preferment [b]. I cannot tell you how sensibly I feel this mark of your goodness, and the infinite obligation you have laid me under by your kind attention, in seeking an opportunity to communicate to me what gives me the highest satisfaction; and, indeed, it gives me very sincere pleasure, not from the smallest idea of personal advantage (as you will readily believe), but I hope it will make him happy, and contribute to give him better health and better spirits; for I know few men I do so much admire, or should love so well, were he even only an acquaintance. For his sake and some others, I like the Chancellorship; but for my own part, the dignity of the Deanship is not the least pleasing. Honour, you know, is the principle of our profession; and if there is any honour in hard knocks, we are likely to have some share: the profit is not yet come to our turn. I cannot omit expressing my obligation

---

[b] His father had, on April 24, 1775, been appointed by Earl Harcourt (then Lord Lieutenant of Ireland), Dean of Emley, county Tipperary, and Chancellor of Dromore, county Down, Ireland, both being ecclesiastical appointments.—(W. J. E.)

to Captain Leveson for the trouble he took in transcribing my father's letter. I am not the less indebted to him that he did it for your sake; and I have no doubt but he rejoices in our good fortune, because it gives you pleasure, and because you have been instrumental in it. It is my sincere prayer that these reciprocal kind offices, which are the marks of confidence and esteem, may long subsist between you, and continue to make you the happiness of each other.

"The 'Charming Nancy,' with Brigadier-General Prescott[c], arrived safe the third instant. By him, George received a gold repeating watch, and a letter from Mrs. Boscawen. I had the pleasure of hearing by him that he had seen her, and that she was in perfect good health. I believe George never neglects to write by every safe opportunity; I never fail to exhort him, though I must do him the justice to say, I believe it is unnecessary.

"In a letter to Mrs. Boscawen shortly after the 19th of April, I hinted to her a desire of looking out for a Lieutenancy to purchase for George in some regiment lately gone home. This desire arose purely from the anxiety and uneasiness I was under all that day lest an unlucky ball should involve us in fresh distress, and complete her misfortunes; and what might we not apprehend, when the most amiable young man I ever knew, Mr. Knight[d], fell by the hands of a rebel? We have since been tolerably quiet; but when the forces from Ireland arrive, we

---

[c] "June 3rd, (1775). This day the 'Lovely Nancy,' who went to England some months ago, returned from there, bringing necessaries for the army; in her came Col. Prescott, now made a Brigadier-General."—*From Journal of a British Officer* (unpublished part), in the possession of Miss Elizabeth Ellery Dana, of Boston.

[d] Lieutenant Joseph Knight, of the 4th Regiment.

shall no doubt commence an active campaign; and though, were he my brother, I should wish him engaged in all the busiest scenes of it, yet knowing how much your mother is wrapped up in him, I confess I cannot be without uneasiness at his being subject to the chance of war; and what could I say to her, should any accident befall her only remaining son? But if you are all satisfied to commit him, I declare I think his present situation the most desirable and most fortunate one he could be thrown into; and you would think so, could you see how much he is improved; and I know he would be far from wishing to exchange it. You are the best judges upon this occasion, and to you I entirely submit it.

"My best wishes and compliments attend you, Captain Leveson, and the young Hero.

"I am, dear Madam, with the truest gratitude and esteem,

"Your ever obliged and obedient servant,

"W. G. EVELYN."

Between the date of the last letter (June 6th), and the next one, to the Honble. Mrs. Leveson Gower (dated Aug. 19th), he no doubt wrote to his father, giving him a full account of the battle of Bunker's Hill, on the 17th of June; for we find that he was so much awakened to the increasing bitterness and intensity of the coming struggle and the fiery ordeal through which he had that day passed, that he wrote his will that same evening; and later on, when the troops were about disembarking, and were off Staten Island (Aug. 20, 1776), he also attached to it a long codicil. Full copies of both of these interesting

Capt. W. G. Evelyn.

documents will be found in the Appendix. Presuming that a letter was written to his father shortly after June 17th, it may have been passed around among the relations and friends of the family in Ireland, and never returned to his father. Many enquiries have been made, but no other letters can be found of Capt. Evelyn's than these embodied in this collection.

It may, however, be opportune to quote here the brief account of the battle of Bunker's Hill, found in the historical record of the 52nd (or Oxfordshire Light Infantry), which regiment played such a distinguished part in the battle, and suffered so severely. William Napier, the historian of the Peninsular War, said of it,—that it was "a regiment never surpassed in arms, since arms were borne by men."

"The Americans were plainly seen at work, throwing up entrenchments around the hill; and preparations were at once made for landing a body of men to dislodge the enemy, and take possession of the works. Ten companies of Grenadiers, ten of Light Infantry, with the 5th, 38th, 43rd, and 52nd regiments, with a proportion of Field Artillery, were detailed for this service. Embarking from Boston in boats, about noon of the 17th of June, the troops crossed the river, and landed on the opposite shore, when they formed immediately; the Light Infantry being posted on the right, and the Grenadiers upon their left. The 5th and 38th drew up in the rear of those corps, and the 43rd and 52nd formed a third line. The ships of war opened their fire upon the enemy's works, and the troops ascended the steep hill, and advanced to storm the entrenchments. The approach to the hill was covered with grass, reaching to the knees, and intersected with walls and fences of various enclosures.

The difficult ascent, the heat of the weather, and the superior numbers of the enemy, and their incessant fire, made the enterprise particularly arduous. The Light Infantry were directed to force the left point of the breastwork, to take the enemy's line in flank; while the Grenadiers were to attack in front, supported by the 5th and 52nd regiments. These orders were executed with perseverance; and notwithstanding the numerous impediments offered, the enemy was forced from his stronghold, and driven from the peninsula, leaving behind five pieces of cannon.

"In this action the 52nd particularly distinguished itself. It suffered, however, severely; the whole of the grenadier company, with the exception of eight men, were either killed or wounded.

"From August 25, 1775, the 52nd regiment was augmented from ten to twelve companies of fifty-six privates each."

The late General Martin Hunter, who was present as an Ensign in the 52nd, writes in his Journal:—"The grenadier and light companies (of the several regiments before enumerated) attacked the breastworks extending from the Charleston heights (or Bunker's Hill) redoubt to the Mystic river; while the remaining companies attacked the redoubt itself. About one hundred yards from the latter, they were stopped by some brick-kilns and enclosures, and exposed for some time to the whole of its fire; and it was here that so many men were lost. The remains of the 52nd regiment continued at the advanced post the whole of the night after the battle; several attacks were made on them during the night, but the Americans were constantly repulsed."

LETTER IX.

To the Honble. Mrs. Leveson Gower, South-street, Grosvenor-square.

"*Boston Camp, August* 19*th*, 1775.

"Dear Madam,—The 'Charming Nancy' returns once more to visit you, and carries with her Mrs. Gage, and others of less note, whose curiosity as to the business of war is, I believe, sufficiently satisfied, and who begin to discover that a winter may be full as agreeable in London as in a town invested on all sides by thousands of armed men, cut off from all resources (I may almost say) by sea as well as by land, and threatened every day to be attacked with fire and sword. With you, who are so jealous of the honour of the British flag, I shall risk my credit, if I tell you what insults have been offered to it with impunity; but indeed they are too many to relate.

"The Yankey fishermen in their whale-boats have repeatedly drove off the stock, and set fire to the houses on islands, under the guns of the fleet. They have killed a midshipman of the Admiral's (Brown), and destroyed the sloop he commanded. They have burned the light-house at the entrance of the harbour, killed Lieutenant Colthurst (who commanded thirty Marines), some of his men, and took the rest prisoners.

"They have burned an armed sloop belonging to the 'Rose' man-of-war, and we hear have taken another, called the 'Diligence,' belonging to the Admiral, and lastly have cut off nine-and-thirty of the 'Falcon's' crew, and have taken all her boats except one; the Lieutenant has made his escape, much wounded. And to complete all, the

Admiral has had a boxing-match in the streets, has got his eyes blackened, and his sword broke by a gentleman of the town, whom he had used very ill, and struck repeatedly, before he returned his blows.

"A few nights ago General Clinton had laid the plan of giving the rebels a general *alerte*, which was to have begun at twelve o'clock, by surprising and attacking all their outposts at the same instant; and the Admiral was at the same time to have made a descent, and burned a small town on the coast. Our part succeeded as well as we could wish, indeed better, for with a few men of our regiment I had the honour of burning an advanced post of the rebels, which was more than was intended in the original plan. The Admiral's part miscarried, but for what reason I do not know. The truth is, there is no good understanding between him and the General, and he endeavours to counteract the General wherever he is concerned. Every man both in the army and navy wishes him recalled, as the service must always suffer where there is such disagreement betwixt the leaders.

"Our situation has undergone very little change since the affair of the 17th of June, except the daily loss of men and officers in the hospitals. I suppose the accounts of that transaction did not meet with credit in England, and that it could not be believed that a thousand men and officers of the bravest troops in the world could in so short a time be cut off by irregulars. After two or three such instances, you good people of old England will find out that five or six thousand men are not sufficient to reduce a country of 1500 miles in extent, fortified by nature, and where every man from fifteen to fifty is either a volunteer, or compelled to carry arms; amongst whom the number of our countrymen is very great, and they are the most dangerous enemies we have to encounter. [The people of England] will find out that some other mode must be adopted than gaining every little hill^e at the expense of a thousand Englishmen; and if they mean to continue masters of this country, they will lay aside that false humanity towards these wretches which has hitherto been so destructive to us. They must lay aside the notion that hurting America is ruining Great Britain, and they must permit us to restore to them the dominion of the country by laying it waste, and almost extirpating [f] the present rebellious race, and upon no other terms will they ever possess it in peace.

"Major Bishop's state of health making it necessary for him to go home, I think I shall take the liberty of troubling him with this letter, though I believe he cannot get a passage in the 'Charming Nancy,' but goes in another which sails at the same time. I fancy George writes by him, and to his information I refer you for particulars as to us and our situation. I dare say this report of George will give you satisfaction. I shall only say in general, that he continues to improve. I dare say you are in some concern for us, from the idea of our being obliged to live upon salt pork and pease. Fresh provision is in general rather scarce, very dear, and not of the best kind; but we come in for a share now and then. We have had a good recruit within these few days; our transports having brought in upwards of two thousand sheep

[e] Alluding to the battle of Bunker's Hill.
[f] In reference to the above passage, great allowance should be generously made for the writer. The expression about "extirpating" is quite unworthy of a brave soldier and a Christian gentleman. It is foreign to the real nature of the writer, who was carried away by his feelings.—(W. J. E.)

from some islands near New York, which is a very seasonable relief to our sick and wounded. George and I come in sometimes for a good dinner among the great people, and are particularly indebted to Lord Percy and General Clinton. We have not the honour of an introduction to General Burgoyne.

"I am strictly enjoined, whenever I write to you, not to omit presenting Adair's most respectful compliments to you and Captain Leveson. He is much taken notice of here, and in great repute from having been one of the first men who entered the enemy's works on the 17th of June. He is strongly recommended for a company, and I hope will get one, as there has been a great mortality among the Marine captains; five or six of them being already dead.

"My best wishes attend you and Captain Leveson, and little family.

"I am, dear Madam,
"With the greatest esteem,
"Your faithful and obedient servant,
"W. G. EVELYN."

LETTER X.

To the Reverend Doctor Evelyn (his Father), Trim, Ireland.

"*Boston Camp, August 19th*, 1775.

"MY DEAR SIR,—I cannot suffer a ship to sail from hence without writing to you, though it should be only half-a-dozen lines to say I am well. A transport sails tomorrow, and takes home Mrs. Gage, some other ladies, and our disabled men. I fancy they will find it full as agreeable to pass the winter in England, as to spend it here upon salt pork and pease.

"We have, however, just now got a recruit of fresh provisions [by] a fleet of transports which were sent to some islands near New York, with about 2,000 sheep and some oxen. These will be of infinite service to our poor sick and wounded people, with whom the hospitals are crowded, and who suffer very much from the flux. We find nothing more difficult to get here than money; none to be had under 15 per cent., and not always even for that, and without it nothing else can be had.

"If a boat, as sometimes happens, comes in with a few half-starved sheep, we must pay a shilling a pound, or eat no mutton. However, we get on, and hope before winter your plentiful country will furnish us abundantly with good beef, and butter, and potatoes. Those who have connections in Cork have sent to their friends for a supply.

"The rebels have got some reinforcements of riflemen from Virginia and Pennsylvania, mostly Irishmen. They have made some little attempts upon our out-parties, without success; and we have taken one or two of them prisoners. We have one of them in jail, whose name is Creuse, [he] comes from the county Westmeath, and says he is related to Miles and Wat Dowdall. I suspect his name to be Dowdall, and that he was Captain of the party, because we know that they were commanded by a man of that name; but he denies being the person, and says he was only a Corporal.

"They are burrowing like rabbits all around us, determined not to leave us a passage through which we may surprise them. We gave them a hearty fright a few nights ago, by attacking their outposts on all quarters at the same instant. It was done with a view of distracting them, whilst the Admiral was to make a descent and burn a little town in the bay; but he miscarried as usual, and the Fleet was once more defeated. On our side we threw them into great confusion, and [I am] convinced, had it been the plan to push [forward] about 2,000 men, we might have got into their very works; but nothing more was intended than to give them a general *alerte*, and to make a diversion. However, I had the good fortune, by pushing forward with about a dozen men, to burn four or five houses in which they kept an advanced post. On General Howe's [side], I am afraid we had a few men wounded by our people, who got into some confusion in the dark. The letters in the enclosed were taken in a sloop, and are worth your reading. I only desire in return that you will send me, from Cork, a cask of beef, another of tongues, two of butter, two of potatoes, and a hogshead of claret, and you will much oblige, &c.

"W. G. E."

LETTER XI.

To the Reverend Doctor Evelyn (his Father), Trim, Ireland.

"*Charlestown, near Boston, October 7th,* 1775, *per General Gage.*

"My dear Sir,—Ships arrive here from Great Britain every week, and bring packets for everybody but me. My good friends, indeed, in England remember me, and frequently send me packets, and other good things; but they also complain that they know as little of you, as if the Atlantic rolled between you. But I shall persevere in letting you hear from me, and hope now and then to extract a letter from you. As I know you like anything better than writing, I am willing to compound with you, and will let you off upon easy terms. I am now so situated, from my recommendations to the general officers, and some little notice they have been pleased to take of me, that I am among the number of those who flatter themselves that some time or other it may be my turn to receive marks of their favour. In the meantime, nothing so much assists one's own endeavours, as to put those gentlemen frequently in mind of one through the means of their own particular friends. Now, my dear Sir, what I would willingly engage you to do for me is, when you find yourself in Dublin, or among any great folks, to remember poor me three thousand miles off, 'my lodging upon the cold ground,' and now and then *ducking* at the whistling of a twenty-four pounder, one of which came a few days ago into our camp, went through one of our tents, and fairly took the crown out of one of the King's Own Grenadiers' hats. His head was not in it. Now, Sir, there's nothing reconciles being shot at to one, so much as being paid for it.

"If, therefore, as I said before, when you get among lords spiritual and temporal, you would cast about, and find out through what channel you could come at General Howe, General Clinton, Lord Percy, General Grant, Colonel Patterson, any General or man of rank who may be coming out, or may hereafter be sent out, you will hardly conceive what importance it is of to one; even the communicating any little news to me either public or private, gives one an appearance of consequence, and is of great advantage. 'Tis inconceivable the trifling circumstances by which one rises in our line. General Howe (upon General Gage's return) being Commander-in-Chief here, has taken an officer [g] of ours to be his aide-de-camp: nobody can tell why. Lord Percy being made a Major-General, has taken another, to the astonishment of everybody; but they have reasons of their own. Among the general officers here, General Howe, General Clinton, and Lord Percy, are particularly civil to me. General Howe is married to a sister of Mr. Conolly's, who is at her brother's in Ireland. In short, Sir, I shall leave the mode to yourself, or to those who can inform you better than I can; nor do I know anybody who could put you in the line so well as your friend Mr. Butler at the Castle, who knows everybody, and their connections.

"There is another point, my dear Sir, upon which I must request of you to exert yourself for me; it is of the most material consequence to me, as this is the period for us soldiers to push our fortunes. Should this war continue a few years longer, new levies must certainly be made. In sixty-two, when five regiments were raised in Ireland, you could have had a company for me by only speaking to a Provost, and I should now certainly be something higher. If another such opportunity should offer, I hope you will not be unmindful of me. I have taken up this profession for life, and it is my business to get on in it as fast as possible. I cannot say I have any great pretensions to more than I have already got, nor have I got more than I have a good right to. There are a number of companies to be raised just now; perhaps when they are complete they may be regimented, but

---

[g] Captain Nisbitt Balfour was made his second aide-de-camp.

I am only alluding to what may happen a year or two hence.

"I am just now encamped on the heights of Charlestown, or Bunker's Hill, the scene of action on the 17th of June. We expect to be pretty late in the field this year, and shall probably not be idle during the winter. The next campaign we shall have something to do, for General Howe will not trifle when he gets reinforcements and proper authority.

"I hope before the end of it to be able to tell you that Boston, New York, Philadelphia, and all the capital towns on the Continent, are but stacks of chimneys like Charlestown here.

"Boscawen is well. The regiment is in camp in Boston; but the Light Infantry company which I command is here. I expect the Grenadiers before Christmas. I beg my love to all at home.

"I am, dear Sir,
"Your most affectionate,
"W. G. E."

LETTER XII.

To the Reverend Doctor Evelyn (his Father), Trim, Ireland.

"*Boston, December* 4, 1775.

"My dear Sir,—As I make it a rule to write to you by every opportunity, notwithstanding I never hear from you,—that is, not above once a-year,—I cannot suffer the 'Boyne' to return without letting you know that we are still in camp; yet we are in tolerable good health and spirits, and not yet so overrun with the scurvy as you would expect of people who live upon salt pork, without roots or vegetables of any kind. The Light Dragoons, and such gentry who have a good deal of money, may now and then get fresh provisions; but your Infantry in general cannot well afford to give eighteen-pence a pound for mutton and bad butter, twelve shillings for a goose, six for a chicken, and twelve shillings for a bushel of potatoes. I am glad, however, there was no beef, butter, or potatoes for me on board the ship that lately came from Cork freighted with these things, and a quantity of claret sent to different officers by their friends in Ireland; for the rebels have taken her with some of their little privateering schooners of four and six guns, who every day insult the British flag with impunity, and who will continue to take every ship that is not either provided for defence, or sent under convoy. We must suppose that all representations sent by the army of the state of this country, are regarded as chimerical or exaggerated. One would think that the taking of Ticonderoga, and June 17, would have put the matter past doubt. But if these are not sufficient, perhaps their being in possession of all Canada except Quebec, (and we are in hourly expectation of hearing that it has surrendered,) the taking some of our transports, and among them a brig loaded with mortars, shells, carcasses, and all kinds of ordnance stores, may open the eyes of the people at home, and convince them that this is a more serious matter than they apprehended.

"This brig, whose safe arrival was of the utmost consequence to us, and whose cargo was of most infinite importance to the rebels, because she contained the very things they were in the greatest need of, and could not be supplied with by any other possible means, was sent from England with other Artillery ships, and she the only one of them without a soldier on board, and totally unprovided with any means of defence. 'Tis said they sailed under the convoy of the 'Phœnix' man-of-war, who quitted them a few days after they left the land. The others are all arrived, and she who was of such consequence to us, we hear is taken, notwithstanding we had several men-of-war out cruising for her; and two of them actually fell in with her, and parted again in a gale of wind. 'Tis impossible to consider the circumstances of this affair, and to call it accident. Surely some inquiry will be made into it, and examples made, for there must be a fault somewhere, and it is a matter of indifference to us whether it is by design or carelessness; the enemy are supplied, so [we] are to be sacrificed by it.

"As they are now enabled to burn Boston, I most sincerely hope they will do it, that we may be enabled to leave it, and transfer the scene to some other part of the Continent. I have lately had some letters from Mrs. Boscawen, so full of distress at her son's situation, that I have solicited General Howe to permit him if possible to go home. He has in the kindest manner in the world appointed him a Lieutenant in the 63rd Regiment, and ordered him home recruiting. We have procured him a passage in the 'Boyne,' which is said to sail to-morrow, and he takes charge of this letter. I shall be exceedingly relieved by having this weighty charge taken off my hands; but I feel more satisfaction in being in the smallest degree instrumental to the comfort and happiness of the best of women, whose goodness to me is more than I can express.

"General Burgoyne goes home in the 'Boyne,' I suppose to lay a state of this country before the nation. He appears, from the line he has taken here, to have been intended rather as a negotiator (had he been admitted to any intercourse) than to be active in the field. He is a man of great abilities, and power of language: his going home is extremely judicious: his representations of affairs will give a great bias. His coadjutors, Howe and Clinton, are certainly two of the first men in our service. It will give you satisfaction to hear that they are both particularly civil to me. I am more immediately under the command of the latter, and have been on one or two little parleys with him, in which he has done me singular honour. Some time ago, he proposed an excursion across the water towards Cambridge, to reconnoitre the rebels' situation, and was pleased to communicate his intention to me the day before, with orders to examine the ground and report to him. We landed next day, with about 200 Light Infantry, on a hill where the rebels had a guard, and having been appointed to command the advanced party, I endeavoured to gain a pass and cut them off; however, they got there before me, and after firing at me from a good distance, retreated, except one man, whom I took prisoner. They fired several cannon-shot at us from their works, and a good deal of small arms from numbers of them that came down towards the pass, which the tide had then overflowed, but without doing any execution, though their shot reached us. We stayed till we did our business, when the men were ordered to re-embark, and I had the honour of being left with thirty men as a rear-guard, till they should be all on board. Orders were then sent to me to retire, which I did very quietly; and when they saw the coast clear they took courage, and ventured over, and threw away a vast deal of ammunition when we were out of their reach. Our people at Charleston and the 'Scarborough' man-of-war fired some round and grape-shot at them with good effect, as we are since told; eight or nine were killed. Our men, in returning to the boats, carried off a dozen head of cattle, which sold for £150. The money was divided among the soldiers and sailors, and General Howe gave them a present of porter. I had the satisfaction of receiving the thanks of both generals in a very pleasing manner, for the little I had to say to the matter. It was very pleasant; a little praise will at any time draw a soldier into a scrape. The hills were crowded with spectators, and we are told it was one of the prettiest sights they ever beheld. What made it most satisfactory was, that we completed our business and returned, without having a man hurt. In a few days we hope to have our works upon this hill (Bunker's Hill) completed, and the barracks fit to receive the Guards. We are then to go into Boston for the winter, leaving 600 men here, to be relieved every fortnight. 'Tis a pity General Gage did not fix some plan for the winter before he went away; our works would have been finished, and we should not have been kept in the field till this season of the year. Those on the Boston side have been in quarters some time. We look every day for the Irish transports: only one of them is arrived, with three companies of the 17th Regiment, among them Captain Lyons; and in his company of Grenadiers is James Lorimer, son of Hugh Lorimer, over the Ban. He is a stout, likely young fellow, and I hope I may have it in my power to be of some service to him. If by one of the many ships that sail from Cork it were practicable to send me a little beef, butter, or potatoes, any of them would be extremely acceptable these hard times.

"I should be glad to hear how the Corporation goes on.

"My love to all friends.

"I am, dear Sir,

"Your most affectionate,

"W. G. EVELYN."

LETTER XIII.

TO THE HONBLE. MRS. LEVESON GOWER, SOUTH-STREET, GROSVENOR-SQUARE.

"*Boston, January* 15*th*, 1776.

"DEAR MADAM. — Some ships will have arrived in England with officers and men from hence, by whom you may probably have expected to receive letters from me; but at the time of their departure I was on a detached duty, which prevented my writing by them. However, the omitting of an opportunity is now of less consequence, as the great object of your solicitude is long since (I hope) safely arrived among you. From the winds we had here about the time of his sailing, we conclude he must have had a very quick passage; and as his coming must have been quite unexpected, I hope he took precautions not to surprise his Mama. I gave him very particular charges on that head, knowing how much she would be affected at his sudden appearance. She must feel great satisfaction at our succeeding as happily in every circumstance as we could wish, and I hope her mind is now perfectly at ease. The arrival of the 'Boyne' will open the eyes of the nation, and we hope great effects from the powers of General Burgoyne. The obstinacy of these people is such, that it is necessary they should feel the severity of punishment, and in the spring we expect to begin with them in earnest. They have gone so far, that they cannot easily recede, and it will require a powerful force to subdue them. The assistance of foreign troops will be highly politick, and of those, Russians are certainly the most eligible, not only as being good soldiers, but by their not having any connections in this country; and from not understanding the language, they are less likely to be seduced by the artifice and intrigue of these holy hypocrites.

"A large force will be necessary, as we shall probably keep three armies on foot: one here, one to the southward, and one in Canada, if we have not entirely lost it; but we imagine General Carlton is still in possession of Quebec, and it is just now reported that he has given the rebels a drubbing, and taken their commander—a Colonel Arnold—prisoner. Brigadier Prescott[h] is taken, and is, with several other officers, prisoner at Albany. Admiral Shuldham[i] is arrived, to the great mortification of Mr. Graves, who most unwillingly resigns to him, and sets out on his return home in a fortnight or three weeks' time. Neither the 'Centurion,' 'Orpheus,' or 'Experiment' have yet appeared. As we have had remarkably violent gales of wind, 'tis thought they may be drove to the West Indies. The last letter I received from Mrs. Boscawen

---

[h] For an account of Brigadier Prescott, see Appendix.
[i] Admiral Molyneux Shuldham, afterwards created Baron Shuldham, of the peerage of Ireland. The title became extinct with him. "Mr. Graves" was Admiral Graves, who arrived at Boston in the "Preston," of 60 guns, on July 1, 1774.

mentions that she had ordered some portable soup, and that Captain Leveson had sent from Plymouth a hogshead of porter and a large cheese for George, which I suppose may be on board one of those ships, as I hear nothing of them from any yet arrived. This instant there is an account of the 'Centurion' lying in the bay, so that 'tis possible the others may not be far off.

"In some former letters, I mentioned the civilities that Generals Howe and Clinton were pleased to shew me, particularly the latter, under whose command I had more particularly enlisted, by changing to the Light Infantry company. He is now ordered on some expedition (report says to the southward); he takes with him only two companies, one of which is mine, granted, as I am told, at his own particular request. The men have been on board a transport for some days, and to-morrow I expect to embark on board the 'Falcon' (Captain Linzee), and sail immediately. The General goes in the 'Mercury,' but sends me in the other, having done me the honour of employing me in a matter of some trust and importance, which I am not at liberty to explain. Diligence and attention shall not be wanting on my part to promote the success of this undertaking, and acquit myself of my small share with credit to myself, and satisfaction to my commanding officer.

"The applications from officers to go upon this expedition are innumerable; not one in the garrison who does not envy my situation. Lord Rawdon [k] (who is very much

---

[k] Then a lieutenant of the grenadier company of the 5th Regiment. Became afterwards Earl of Moira and Marquis of Hastings. He distinguished himself in the south by his command of the troops until the arrival of Lord Cornwallis. He was Governor-General of India for nine years. He died at Malta in 1826.

my friend) has, with some difficulty, obtained leave to go as an extra aide-de-camp. We promise ourselves we shall have a pleasant party, and perhaps do good service. Boston we bid adieu to, and only desire to hear that

"Grass may grow where Troy town stood."

Indeed, it is fast approaching to that state; for every regiment furnishes a constant working party of twenty men, who are employed in pulling down houses, and piling the wood for firing, which gives us hopes that in a short time this hotbed of rebellion will be reduced to a very narrow compass.

"The theatre flourishes surprisingly, and has brought forth some very capital performers. We were most ridiculously interrupted a few nights ago, just as they were going to begin 'The Blockade of Boston,' a performance of General Burgoyne, taking off the figures and manner of the Yankee soldiers, and by all accounts a very laughable thing[1]. The 'Busy Body' was ended, and every one

---

[1] "It was about the same time that a large assembly, determined to keep their spirits up, were collected to enjoy the sport of a farce, said to be written by General Burgoyne (previous to his Saratoga expedition, of course), in which General Washington, now commanding at Cambridge, as the hero, was dressed in an uncouth style, with a large wig and long rusty sword, attended by his orderly sergeant, in his country dress, having on his shoulder a rusty firelock, 7 or 8 feet long. At the moment this figure appeared on the stage, one of the regular sergeants came running on behind him, who threw down his bayonet, and shouted, 'The Yankees are attacking our works on Bunker Hill!' (This was after the battle.) Some of the audience considered it a part of the play, but were undeceived by hearing General Howe cry out, 'Officers, to your alarm posts!' when all was confusion and dismay, and the gay congregation dispersed in the twinkling of an eye."—*Traits of the Tea Party* (*Boston*), being a Memoir of Geo. R. T. Hawes, p. 211.

From the late General Martin Hunter's Journal:—"During the

waiting with impatience for the curtain to be drawn up, when we were alarmed with the report of firing; upon which we all turned out, went to our respective posts, and cursed the Yankees for spoiling our entertainments. A few impertinent fellows, it seems, under cover of the night, stole into Charlestown, and set fire to two or three deserted, half-demolished houses; upon which our people fired some shots at them from the works, which disturbed us, and obliged us fairly to raise the siege. If *that* was their intention, they deserve some credit for timing it so well; 'tis probable it was, for they cannot stand ridicule.

"We are threatened with Sir J. Amherst [m]; the army do

---

winter, plays were acted at Boston twice a-week, by the officers and some ladies. A farce called the 'Blockade of Boston,' written by General Burgoyne, was acted. The enemy knew the night it was to be performed, and made an attack on the mill at Charleston at the very hour the farce began; they fired some shots, and surprised and carried off a sergeant's guard. We instantly turned out, and manned the works; and a shot being fired by one of our advanced sentries, a firing commenced at the redoubt, and could not be stopped for some time. An orderly sergeant standing outside the play-house door, who heard the firing, immediately running into the play-house, got upon the stage, crying out, 'Turn out! turn out! they're hard at it, hammer and tongs.' The whole audience, supposing the sergeant was acting a part in the farce, loudly applauded; and there was such a noise, he could not for some time make himself heard. When the applause was over, he again cried out, 'What the d———l are ye about? If ye won't believe me, ye need only go to the door, and there ye'll hear and see both.' If the enemy intended to stop the farce, they certainly succeeded, as the officers immediately left the play-house, and joined their regiments."—Quoted in *History of the 52nd Regiment.*

[m] In February, 1775, the British Government determined to raise the army in Boston to 10,000 men, and supersede General Gage. The service was offered to General Jeffery Amherst, but declined, unless the army should be raised to 20,000 men. Sir William Howe was then appointed. The threatened infliction of Sir J. Amherst perhaps

not like it. They wish to remain as they are; but if it is to be, I shall hope for your good word. My best respects wait on Mrs. Boscawen, and Captain Leveson, and my friend George. His old school-fellow, Barker, will this day be a Captain in the 10th Regiment.

"Till I can inform you where I am to be found, I shall hope to receive your letters directed, as usual, to Boston.

"I am, Madam,
"Your ever obliged,
"W. G. EVELYN."

LETTER XIV.

To the Reverend Doctor Evelyn (his Father), Trim, Ireland[n].

"*Boston, January* 15*th*, 1776.

"MY DEAR SIR,—I have delayed writing to you to the last moment, that I might be able to inform you of a circumstance that I hope will give you pleasure. I have before told you that upon two or three little occasions, I have had the good fortune to recommend myself to the notice of General Clinton. He is now going upon some expedition[o] (common fame says to Virginia), and

---

alludes to the report of some fresh change in the command of the troops. Sir J. Amherst was a Knight of the Order of the Bath, and was created on his return to England a peer of the realm, as Lord Amherst.

[n] Dean Evelyn died at Dublin, March, 1776.

[o] To Carolina. "The expedition to the Carolinas never met the approval of Howe, who condemned the activity of the southern governors, and would have them avoid all disputes till New York should be recovered. When Lord Dunmore learned from Clinton

takes two companies of Light Infantry to attend him. He has been pleased to choose mine and the 44th; they are already on board a transport, and I expect we shall sail to-morrow. The General goes in the 'Mercury,' and has ordered me on board the 'Falcon' sloop-of-war, on a private expedition of consequence and trust, and which, from the discretionary powers given to me, is highly honourable and flattering. And now for a little good fortune at setting out! It shall not be my fault if I do not *parvenir*. Lord Rawdon[p] goes with the General, about his person; he is very much distinguished here as a most promising young man in the military line, and I am flattered to think I hold some place in his good opinion. If from your acquaintance with Lord and Lady Moira you could procure me any further recommendations to him, I should be much obliged to you.

"I have hardly time to desire to be recommended to my friends, or to say how much

"I am, dear Sir,

"Your affectionate,

"W. G. EVELYN."

that Cape Fear river was the place appointed for the meeting of the seven regiments from Ireland, he broke out into angry complaints, that no heed had been paid to his representations, his sufferings, and his efforts; that Virginia, 'the first on the continent for riches, power and extent,' was neglected, and the preference given to 'a poor insignificant colony' where there were no pilots, nor a harbour that could admit half the fleet, and where the army, should it land, must wade for many miles through a sandy pine barren, before it could reach the inhabited part of the country."—*Bancroft*.

[p] Lord Rawdon, afterwards the Earl of Moira, died at Malta, in 1826.

THE HON.BLE M.RS (FRANCES) BOSCAWEN.
BORN 1719.   DIED 1805.
FROM A PORTRAIT AT WOTTON, PAINTED BY RAMSEY.

CAPT. W. G. EVELYN. 83

LETTER XV.

To the Honourable Mrs. Boscawen, Colney Hatch, Middlesex.

"*New York Island, September* 24*th*, 1776.

"Dear Madam.—Captain Balfour q of our regiment, aide-de-camp to General Howe, has promised to charge himself with any letter I may have to send to England, and should I have an opportunity of seeing him before his departure, I shall enjoin him to wait upon you to give you any information you may be desirous of hearing, of our situation and the state of affairs here. He carries home the accounts of our getting possession of New York, which, by a masterly stroke of General Howe, was effected without the loss of a man, except two or three Hessians, who were killed through their own faults. From the time of our driving the rebels out of Long Island, they daily expected an attack upon York, and had so strengthened themselves with batteries and breast-works, that they looked upon a landing as impracticable.

q Captain Nisbitt Balfour, of the 4th Foot, was one of the executors of Captain Evelyn's will. He commanded the "Queen's Guards," sent to protect the loyalists of Marshfield, Massachusetts, in December, 1774, by General Gage. General Gage's return of the loss at Bunker's Hill, includes Captain Balfour as wounded. He was subsequently stationed at New York, and while there (see Historical Magazine, vol. ii. p. 183, 1858), he told an American prisoner (who had known Captain Balfour at Marshfield), "that he came out of the fight at Charleston with only five men following him, while he had entered it with a full company." He was second aide-de-camp to General Howe, and was made a major whilst in England, Nov. 19, 1776, and returned to the seat of war not very long afterwards. He was made Lieutenant-Colonel, and commanded at Charleston, South Carolina, in 1781.

By the disposition General Howe had made of the troops, they were deceived as to the place where he intended to make his attack. On the night of the 14th, the boats were sent quietly up the river to a creek, opposite to which five men-of-war were stationed. We marched at the same time, and embarked in the morning. We rowed a considerable way up the river, higher than where we were to land, and made fast the boats to some transports till the whole should come up, by which the rebels were still deceived, and drew themselves up in their works to receive us. On a certain signal we all pushed off together, and at the same instant the men-of-war began such a fire as nothing could withstand. The Light Infantry, in the headmost boats, gained a high and steep rock, which they ascended, and secured a safe landing for the rest of the troops. They were followed by the Grenadiers, Hessians, and Artillery, and afterwards by the body of the army. The rebels, upon the firing of the ships (which is not to be described), and upon seeing the troops gain the shore, fled in the greatest confusion. Their garrisons in New York abandoned it with the utmost precipitation, leaving their forts, their cannon, and a quantity of military stores, and that evening a brigade of ours took possession of the town. We advanced two or three miles, the rebels retiring before us, till they left us the ground which the General wished to occupy, which is a strong pass between the north and east rivers, about seven miles from New York. The rebels are on the opposite hills, and extend from thence to Kingsbridge, burying themselves in entrenchments, in which they place their only security. The taking of the island and town of New York without any loss, though above fifty thousand men were prepared to defend them, must be considered as a consummate piece of generalship; and the execution of it, between the amazing fire from the shipping, the confusion and dismay of the rebels, the Light Infantry clambering up the steep and just accessible rocks, the water covered with boats full of armed men pressing eagerly towards the shore, was certainly one of the grandest and most sublime scenes ever exhibited. This easy victory was not sufficient to satisfy the eagerness and impetuosity of our men. The next day, a few companies of Light Infantry were prompted to attack a party of the rebels, and with more ardour than discretion, pushed them to their very lines, where they were supported by their cannon, and by three or four thousand men. This obliged us to support our people, and brought on a skirmish, in which we had nine or ten men killed, a few officers and about ninety men wounded, and [which] answered no other end than to prove our superiority even in their beloved woods, as the ground we gained we did not want, but went back at night to that we had left in the morning. But what will the abettors of American Rebellion say, when they hear that a few nights after their friends had abandoned New York, the emissaries of General Washington, or those left in the town [r] for that purpose,

[r] "Mr. David Grim, a merchant of New York, who saw the conflagration, has left a record of the event. He says the fire broke out in a low groggery, a wooden building on the wharf near Whitehall Slip. It was discovered between one and two in the morning of the 21st of September. The wind was from the S.W. But few inhabitants remained in the city, and the flames spread rapidly for awhile unchecked. About 493 houses out of 4000 in the city were consumed. The Tories and the British writers of the day attempted to fix the crime of incendiarism upon the Whigs, but could not. It was well known that the fire had an accidental origin, yet British historians continue to reproduce the libel."—*From Lossing's Field-Book of the Revolution*, vol. ii. p. 819.

with fanatic rage set it on fire in three places, and notwithstanding the endeavours of the troops and many of the inhabitants, it continued to burn till the next afternoon, by which one-third of that beautiful town is consumed. *They* may dignify it with the name of heroism and virtue, but to *us* it will ever appear the excess of villainy even in the virtuous Mr. Washington. And when the conduct of our General toward the town and people of Boston is compared with this action, it must strongly mark the different characters of the two nations, as well as of the individuals who are the actors in this civil war.

"Since the skirmish on the 16th, nothing worth mentioning has happened, except that yesterday three men-of-war were ordered to attack a battery of theirs called Pauli's Hook, and some troops were at the same time embarked in order to be under cover of their fire. Upon the ships appearing before the work, the rebels ran away, and our men are now in possession of it. Having now cleared all the little obstacles out of our way, we expect that another grand stroke will take place before winter, which will not only clear this island of the rebels, but probably disperse the great numbers they have collected; which, once done, the game is up, for they never will assemble again, many of them being compelled to serve, and the greater part of them heartily sick of this business, as appears by their crowding in to us every day.

"One of their Generals (Sullivan), who was taken on the 27th, got permission to go to the Congress, to negotiate an exchange of himself for General Prescott[8], in consequence of which General Prescott is expected in to-day. After Mr. Sullivan had been at the Congress,

---

[8] General Prescott was exchanged for General Charles Lee.

they sent three deputies, Adams, Franklin, and Rutledge, to treat with Lord Howe about an accommodation; but as they set out with 'the Independent States of America,' they were dismissed without listening to any further insolence.

"I must acknowledge that I have received a letter from my friend George[†], which I have not answered, but firmly propose it when I have sufficient time and paper. When Captain Balfour explains to him our situation on the advanced post of the army, he will excuse

---

[†] The only surviving son of Admiral Boscawen. Admiral the Honourable Edward Boscawen, third son of the first Lord Falmouth, was born in Cornwall, August 19, 1711. He entered the Navy at an early age, and was promoted to the rank of Captain in 1737. In 1739 he commanded the "Shoreham," and distinguished himself at the taking of Porto Bello. He was returned to Parliament for Truro in 1741, and represented that borough until the day of his death. In 1742 he married Frances Evelyn Glanville. He commanded the "Dreadnought," of sixty guns, in 1744, greatly distinguishing himself in the years 1746 and 1747, and rose rapidly in the service. In 1751 he became a Lord of the Admiralty; in 1758 he commanded the naval forces at the reduction of Louisburg and St. John. On his return to England he received the thanks of the House of Commons, and was made a Privy Councillor. He rendered most efficient service in many engagements with the French during the years 1758 and 1760, and again received the thanks of Parliament. He died January 10, 1761, at Hatchlands, near Guildford, Surrey, and was buried in the family vault, church of St. Michael, Penkivel, Cornwall, near Tregothnan, the seat of the Falmouth family. His widow, whose published letters to Mrs. Delany shew her to have been a lady of great refinement and considerable literary ability, erected a handsome memorial to his memory in the church of St. Michael. Horace Walpole styled Admiral Boscawen "the most obstinate of an obstinate family;" but Lord Chatham, who must have had better means of appreciating his character, passed this handsome eulogium upon him: "When I apply to other officers respecting any expedition I may chance to project, they always raise objections and difficulties: Boscawen always finds expedients."

me a little longer. I own I often congratulate myself that he is not with me. I beg to be remembered to him, and to present my best respects to my good Mrs. Leveson, and the House of Badminton [u].

"I am, my dear Madam, with the highest respect,
"Your ever obliged and humble servant,
"W. G. EVELYN."

The following Letter was probably the last received by Mrs. Evelyn from her son. The Letter is much worn and soiled, as if his mother had often recurred to it in after years. In a few places it is difficult to decipher.

LETTER XVI.

To MRS. EVELYN (HIS MOTHER), TRIM, IRELAND.

New York Island, Sept. 25*th*, 1776.

"MY DEAR MADAM,—If you have not received a letter which I wrote to you the beginning of August, by a ship bound to Cork, you will be at a loss to account for my being so long silent. In that letter I requested you would draw upon our agents (Adair and Bullock) in London for £40 sterling, which I have in their hands, and which I have not any immediate occasion for. If you have not al[ready] re[ceived] it, I must beg that you will, and not deny me this mark of your confidence in my disposition to afford you every assistance in my power. I only wish

[u] Mrs. Leveson's younger sister Elizabeth was married to Henry, fifth Duke of Beaufort, and resided at Badminton House, Gloucestershire.

I could supply all your wants with that liberality you have ever shewn towards me, and in some degree make lighter your weight of affliction [v], which is almost too heavy for you to bear. What I can do to alleviate it shall never be wanting, and your own piety and virtue will support you under it with fortitude and resignation. Since my last letter to you, we have had an action with the rebels, in which we totally defeated them, with great loss on their parts and very little on ours, and drove them entirely off Long Island. The part of the army in which I am was chiefly engaged. I was lucky enough to come off unhurt, but had six of my men killed and wounded. Those who escaped of the rebels retired to New York. On the 15th of this month, we attacked that island in our boats; and notwithstanding they expected our coming, we landed under cover of the men-of-war, without losing a man, drove the rebels in great confusion to the further end of the island, and now keep possession of York and the country seven miles from it. A few nights after we took it, some villains, wh[o lurked] in town for that purpose, set it on fire in several places, by which about one-third of it was consumed [x]. I am a good deal at

[v] Alluding to the death of his father, the Very Rev. Dean of Emley, which event took place March 28, 1776, at Dublin, about six months before the date of this letter.

[x] See Note to Letter XV. "In the lately-published 'Campaign of 1776 around New York and Brooklyn,' by Henry P. Johnston (3rd vol. of Long Island Historical Society's Memoirs), the following account is given of the capture of an American patroling party of five officers, on the morning of the 27th of August, 1776, the day of the battle of Long Island : 'Captain William Evelyn, "a gallant officer" of the 4th Infantry, or King's Own, and a descendant of the eminent John Evelyn, of England, led the British advance this night ; and it fell to his fortune to surround and capture all five American officers, and send them immediately to Clinton, who commanded the leading

a loss how to direct to you, but shall send it, as the last, to Mr. Reynolds, at Trim. My best love to my aunt. Be assured I shall omit no opportunity of writing to you, and of proving how truly

"I am, my dear Madam,
"Your dutiful and affectionate son,
"W. G. EVELYN."

Copy of the Will of Captain William Glanville Evelyn.

"*Boston June* 17th 1775.

"As all Men who have taken upon them the profession of Arms, hold their Lives by a more precarious tenure than any other Body of People; and as the fatal experience of this Day shews us how particularly it is the case of those who are engaged in war, even with the most despicable Enemy, I think it the Duty of every Man who cares a farthing about the disposal of His affairs, to declare in what manner He wishes to have them disposed of: and tho' all my Worldly Substance is worth very little, yet it is my desire that Peggie Wright^y shall inherit every-

column.' The authority for this statement is a letter from the Honble. Mrs. Boscawen to Mrs. Delany, in the Autobiography of the latter, dated Oct. 17, 1776, which reads: 'We have had a letter from Captain Evelyn, from the field of battle; he was in ye brigade of light infantry, and took 5 officers prisoners, who were sent to observe our motions.' Mr. Johnston attributes the overwhelming defeat of our army at Long Island to the capture of this party, to whom Putnam and Sullivan looked for information of the advance of the British through Jamaica Pass. Captain Evelyn was mortally wounded at the skirmish at Throg's Neck, on the 18th of October, 1776."— From the *Pennsylvania Magazine of History and Biography*, No. viii. p. 473.

^{y} Peggie Wright was a servant in the family of Dr. William Evelyn, between whom and Captain Evelyn an attachment had sprung up, thing I leave behind me; paying out of what may arise from the sale of such things, as she may choose to sell, & little Debts I may owe in *this* country, such as Higgs's money, and a trifle to Mr. Forrest for Linnen, and something we owe Him, Beef, & Potatoes & five Bushels of Oats. I desire her also to pay my servant Sturgess, two Guineas, which Legacy should have been more proportioned to what I owe him for his attachment & fidelity to me, but that what I give to Him, I must take from her. If he should be in my debt upon the Books I desire He may be forgiven.

"The same cause prevents me from taking Notice of some of my Friends in the Regiment for whom I have a very sincere Esteem. I have further to desire, that if my Books should be sold, the three vol^s. of Hudibrass in French and English, the Legacy of my amiable and unfortunate Friend Joe Knight, may be reserved and by some means transmitted to my Father. Whatever Debts I may owe in England or Ireland are very trifling, only to Taylors & Shoemakers, and these I hope my Father will be so good as to discharge, which will be no great addition to the little expence I have ever put him to.

"I am unacquainted with the form of Wills, but this I mean to be my last will & Testament, having never made any other, and I request that Captain Balfour, Capt. Cochrane, Mr. Champagné or any of them, will be kind enough to see the intention of it executed. Given

whilst he was at home on half-pay. She followed him to Boston; and when the British evacuated that city, she went with Captain Evelyn to Halifax, and remained there after his departure for New York. She was, in all probability, summoned to his bed-side after he was wounded, on the 18th of Oct., 1776, to remain until his death on Nov. 6th.

under & written with my own Hand, at Boston Camp this 17th day of June 1775.

"(*Signed*) W. G. EVELYN,
"Captn. 4th Reg^t."

Memorandums.

"*Staten Island Augt. 20th* 1776.

"Upon my going to Carolina in January last I left a paper with Peggie Wright in Boston purporting that in case of my Death it was my desire she should become possessed of whatever property or Effects I might have in America. As she is now in Halifax, I think it necessary to leave a Memorandum with the Regiment to the same effect, but more Explicit.

"The 24th December last I had a Ballance in the Agents' hands of Forty pounds, some shillings, exclusive of my arrears and division of Non Effective Fund. I have in a Letter authorized my Mother to draw on the Agents for the Forty pounds, but am not certain if she will do it. My pay, arrears &c. from that time to this is in the hands of the Agents.

"From the Pay Master of the Regiment, I have drawn on account of my Company, up to the 24th April last about Four hundred Dollars or £93 ,, 6 ,, 8 which by a rough calculation is near their Subsistance to that time, leaving as much in his hands, as we supposed would amount to their Provision Money. There is now in his hands upwards of Four months' pay of my Company, besides Augmentation Money and the Bounty of Eight

Drafts, and one Recruit (Richardson) whom I enlisted. He, not having paid anything, upon my account that I know of, except Nine or Ten Pounds to M^r. Fish.

"In a trunk on board of the 'Sovereign,' Victualler (where most of my Baggage is), I have left in Gold, Ten half Johannes, in Silver One hundred and Forty-six Dollars & four Crown pieces. The accounts of my Company are settled up to the 24th of June, since which settlement they have received a good deal of Money & necessarys from me which are not charged, there is however a Considerable Ball^{ce} due to them, but far short of what I have a demand upon the Paymaster for. Of the Money in my Trunk Twenty Pounds Sterling is due to Captⁿ. Tallemacke, of the 'Scorpion,' or his Agent Mr. McKnight, for a Puncheon of Rum which I've had no opportunity of paying for, since I received the money, I am also indebted to Capt. Drummond for two pieces of Osnaburgh. I recollect nothing else.

"The foregoing being a General Sketch of the State of my affairs, it is my wish that in Case of my Death, my Baggage (of which there is a considerable heap, such as it is) & Effects may be sold, and the money arising therefrom as well as all debts and Balances due to me may be paid to the above mentioned Peggie Wright, excepting only Five Guineas which I desire may be paid to my Servant Sturgess, over & above what wages I may owe him, as a small but gratefull acknowledgement for his fidelity. I also desire that he may have all my silver Shoe and Knee Buckles & my Stock Buckles, and I would wish to recommend him to some good Master as Govr. Martin or Lord Rawdon, who might be better able to reward his services. Whatever money of mine may be in the Agents hands, it's my desire that it may be paid to my Mother, thro' the hands of Mrs. Boscawen or Mrs. Leveson Gower, first paying out of it Nine pounds one shilling to M^r. Busher, which I owe him for Cloth, and is the only Debt I can think of, which comes within my ability to pay. In case my Mother should not be alive, or through any other Cause should not receive this Money, I desire it may be paid to the above mentioned Peggie Wright. I would willingly give some of my acquaintances tokens of the very sincere regard & esteem, I have for them, but if I left them anything I must take so much from her. I only beg that my amiable Friend Captain Knight will accept of the Ring left me by his incomparable and dearly beloved Brother. Given under my Hand at Staten Island, August 20th, 1776.

"(*Signed*) W. G. EVELYN,
"*Cap^n. 4th Reg^t.*"

"I, Joseph Galloway Esquire, Superintendent General of the City of Philadelphia and its Environs, do hereby Certifie unto all, whom it may concern, That the foregoing Pages Numbered 1, 2, 3, 4, 5, 6, contain true and exact Copies of the Probate taken by and before John Potts Esquire, of the last Will and Codicil of William Glanville Evelyn, my Certificate respecting the Right and Power of the said John Pott's Esquire, to take such Probate before him and of the said last Will and Testament and Codicil or addition to such last Will, which said several Copies I have carefully examined and compared with the respective Originals. Given under my Hand at Philadelphia, this Eighth Day of March, in the year of our Lord, 1778.

"J. GALLOWAY,
"*Superintendent General.*"

The foregoing Will of Captain Evelyn's is a careful transcript of a certified copy, which has been preserved through all the changes of time since the Revolution, and was originally destined to be placed in the hands of the Evelyn family in Ireland. It never, however, reached their hands, and its existence was entirely unknown to the family in England, until it was found in the valuable collection of Mr. T. Baily Myers, of New York, who has generously placed a copy of it at my disposal, for which kind courtesy, I desire to express my thanks.

It is much to be regretted that the Probate mentioned above by Mr. J. Galloway, of Philadelphia, has been detached from the above Will, and lost.

The following Letter of young Ensign Evelyn, is the only one that has been preserved, which was written during the seven years' war in Germany. He was at that time about nineteen years of age.

To the Rev. Mr. Evelyn (his Father), at his House in White Friars-street, Dublin.

"*Camp at House, Hanover, July* 17, 1761.

"Dear Sir.—I received your letter about a fortnight ago, since which time I have not had the least opportunity of writing. We were then on the march. I have continued moving ever since. We have just this moment returned from singing *Te Deum* for a victory obtained over the French yesterday, the particulars of which I do not know, but shall refer you to the newspapers; all I know is, that Lord Grantley's corps, consisting of the British Grenadiers, two battalions of Highlanders, and four regiments of Infantry, cannonaded them on the left from four in the morning till about twelve. While the hereditary Prince with his corps engaged them on the right, the other two brigades of British, of which ours is one, were in the centre, and were ordered to line the hedges, which we did, but the French being beat back, we lay very quiet and did not fire a shot. In the morning we marched back, and encamped on the ground we left the night before. The Grenadiers have taken fifteen pieces of cannon, one of them 16 pounds, and four 4-pounders. We have not yet heard how many men are taken or killed on either side. In your letter you are pleased to give me a great deal of merit to which I have not the least title, as my preferment was in turn, and merely owing to my good luck, and not to any particular merit of mine. I enquired for Mr. Conolly; he came over to this country a volunteer. He was never attached to any particular regiment, sometimes with a regiment of Infantry, sometimes with the Artillery. At length, one night in the city of Osnaburg, being in company with some Bombardiers of the Artillery, he was murdered. This is the account I have heard of him, from an officer who knew him. I shall leave it to your better judgment to disclose it to his mother.

"The post is going out, and I have not time to write as much as I could wish, but I shall be much obliged to you if you'll send me a little money, and the sooner the better, as I am really tired of walking all the campaign, which as yet has been very severe. By writing to our agent, Mr. Richardson, in Downing-street, Westminster, he will remit any sum you please to send. Our paymaster has offered to give me any money I should want, but I did not choose to take up any without being certain of having it in my power to pay him again. Besides, I think myself too much in debt already, as I have two commissions to pay for, an ensigncy and lieutenancy. My first ensigncy I have paid for, but on the death of his late majesty, we all got new commissions, which I have to pay for, besides my lieutenancy, which will come to between nine and ten pounds.

"The man waits for my letter. I beg my respects to all friends, my duty to my Mother, and love to John[z].

"I am, dear Sir,
"Your affectionate Son,
"WM. GLANVILLE EVELYN."

With the tender and touching letter of September 25, 1776, to his mother, the correspondence ended by the premature death of the writer, who, it may be observed, is not the only member of the family of Evelyn whose fortunes have been connected with America. Very early in the colonization of the country, Robert Evelyn, the great-great-grand-uncle of Captain Evelyn, embarked about the year 1609 for Virginia, upon a voyage of adventure, and was followed by his youngest son, Robert, the author of the "Letters, &c.," who eventually died in the West Indies. George, supposed to be the elder brother of Robert the younger, is also found in the year 1637 in Maryland, assisting his friend Leonard Calvert, the Governor, in the administration of the colony. More recently, William Evelyn, an officer in the British Army, and an uncle of the present possessor of Wotton, lost his life by shipwreck on the island of Cape Breton, Canada, 22nd of October, 1805.

[z] "John" was his younger brother, the grandfather of the present head of the Evelyn family, at Wotton.

APPENDIX.

COLONEL CLEAVELAND [a], of the Royal Artillery, had a local rank of Brigadier. He and Col. Pattison were in command of the artillery in Boston. The 1st, 3rd, and 4th battalions of the artillery were engaged at Bunker's Hill. When the British troops, under Lieut.-Col. Smith, commenced retiring from Concord on Lexington, they were met by a reinforcement under Lord Percy, accompanied by two field-guns. This was the first appearance of the Royal Artillery in the war. Under the fire of the guns, the troops were able to continue their retreat comparatively unmolested; but before they reached Boston, they had sustained a loss of no less than 273 killed, wounded, and prisoners. Effective as the fire of the English guns was, complaints were made, probably in self-defence, by the commanding officer of the troops, that the artillery were inadequately supplied with ammunition on the occasion. A strong remonstrance was immediately addressed by Col. Cleaveland to the Master General of the Ordnance, stating the true facts:—

"I find it has been said in England, that ammunition was wanting for the two guns which went with the brigade to Lexington,—that they had only 24 rounds per gun. I had a wagon with 140 rounds on the parade, and Lord Percy refused to take it, saying it might retard their march, and that he did not imagine there would be any occasion for more than there was on the side-boxes."

[a] "Col. Cleaveland of the Artillery," p. 35.

APPENDIX. 99

In the batteries on Copp's Hill, and with the guns actually on the field, five companies of the 4th battalion of Royal Artillery were present (Bunker's Hill), viz., Nos. 1, 2, 4, 5, and 8.

Eight field-pieces were actually in action, but twelve accompanied the attacking force: four light 12-pounders, four $5\frac{1}{2}$-inch howitzers, and four light 6-pounders. The attack was made under the fire of the guns. "The troops advancing slowly, and halting at intervals, to give time for the artillery to produce some effect"—(*General Stedman's Journal*). "During the engagement (writes Stedman) a supply of ball for the artillery, sent from the Ordnance department in Boston, was found to be of larger dimensions than fitted the calibres of the field-pieces that accompanied the detachment; an oversight which prevented the use of the artillery."

In opposition to this statement, Colonel Cleaveland's report to the Master General may be quoted: "At Bunker's Hill, I sent 66 rounds to each gun, and not more than half was fired."—(From MSS. in the Royal Artillery Record Office). "Had the reason been that given by Stedman, Colonel Cleaveland was too truthful a man to omit mentioning it. The battle of Bunker's Hill was the 'Inkermann of the American War.' The British loss was 1,054 killed and wounded. The loss of the artillery was small; some 9 or 10 wounded, officers included, and none killed, according to the battalion records. At the battle of Brandywine, Col. Cleaveland distinguished himself, and was duly noticed in a dispatch of Sir William Howe's to Lord George Germaine: 'Much credit is due to Brigadier-General Cleaveland, and to the officers and men of the corps of artillery.' While in Philadelphia, Col. Cleaveland was superseded by Col. Pattison, who commanded the artillery when the British took possession of the Fort of Red Bank. General Pattison was afterwards commandant of the city of New York."

The above account has been condensed from the "History of the Royal Artillery," by Major Duncan, R.A.

Brigadier-General RICHARD PRESCOTT[b], the commanding-officer of the British troops at Newport, Rhode Island, had made himself especially odious to the inhabitants by many acts of petty tyranny and oppression. At last a plan was concocted, and successfully carried out by Lieut.-Col. Barton, of Providence, of capturing him, and carrying him into the American lines on the night of the 10th of July, 1777. Full particulars of this well-contrived and daring enterprise will be found in Lossing's "Field Book of the Revolution," vol. ii. pp. 75, 76. Two popular ballads were also made upon this successful exploit, which are preserved in Duyckinck's "Cyclopædia of American Literature," vol. i. pp. 451, 452.

Extracts from Journals of Congress.

"Resolved, That General Prescott be committed to, and kept in close confinement in, the jail of Philadelphia, till further orders from Congress.

"N.B.—This was occasioned by the cruel and inhuman treatment of Col. Ethan Allen, and the prisoners taken with him near Montreal, by loading them with heavy irons, and, in the most severe weather, keeping them almost naked, and without anything to lie on but bare

[b] "My old friend Col. Prescott," p. 34.

BRIGADIER GENERAL RICHARD PRESCOTT.

boards, which treatment was continued all the time that they were confined in Pendennis Castle in England.

"January 30. Resolved, That Dr. Cadwallader and Dr. Shippen, jun., be desired to inspect the room of the jail where General Prescott is confined, and inquire into the state of his health, and report thereon to Congress.

"February 13. Resolved, That Captain Gordon, upon giving his parole, be permitted, while he remains in town, to visit General Prescott at proper seasons.

"April 9. That Brigadier-General Prescott, upon subscribing the parole ordered, be enlarged from his present confinement."

Extract from a Letter from the "London Chronicle."

"*January* 14—16, 1777.

"An officer who was taken prisoner by the Americans at St. John's, is lately arrived in England. He was a prisoner in Philadelphia with General Prescott and several other officers, and says that, as a party of them were one day dining with General Prescott, a Provincial Captain with thirty soldiers came into the room, and said he was ordered by the Congress to carry General Prescott immediately to the common jail. The General, with the greatest composure, submitted to his fate. The room in which they lodged him was cold and damp, bare walls, no fireplace, the furniture nothing but a chair and a truckle-bed. From the unwholesomeness of this situation and other hardships, the wounds he had received in former services broke out afresh, and reduced him to so low a state, that his death seemed inevitable. Major Preston, who was also a prisoner, went to Hancock, the

President of the Congress, and told him, that if they were determined to sacrifice his brother-officer to their resentment, it would be an act of humanity to dispatch him immediately, and not suffer him to linger in misery. Upon this representation, Dr. Cadwallader[c] was sent to visit him, who, by his humane account of the General's case, and other kind offices, obtained leave for his removal to his former lodgings in the town, with sentinels to guard him. This severe treatment, the Congress declared, was intended as a retaliation for the imprisonment of Ethan Allen, which, though really done by General Carleton's orders, they ascribed to General Prescott, who might have obtained a much more speedy release, by declaring that the orders came from his superior officer; but at that juncture Montgomery was carrying on the siege of Quebec, and General Carleton seemed in danger of falling into the hands of Congress; therefore General Prescott, though formally interrogated by deputies from the Congress on the subject, resolutely suffered them to continue under the mistake, till Montgomery was defeated and Quebec secure. The above particulars were related by an officer, who was at dinner with the General when he was taken into custody."

General Prescott was exchanged in April, 1778, for General Charles Lee.

The capture of General Lee by Lieut.-Col. WILLIAM

[c] Extract from a Letter in the "New York Gazette," Nov. 25, 1776:— "When Mr. Cadwallader, a young officer in the service of the rebels, was dismissed the other day by the General's orders, on account of his father's civil treatment of General Prescott while a prisoner, he burst into tears upon the instances of generosity shewn him, and discovered such sensibility on the occasion, as did him honour as a man and a gentleman. 'Tis to be regretted that such a man could be in rebellion against his king and the constitution of his country."

Painted by H. Edridge 1818   Engraved by S.W. Reynolds Bayswater

The Right Honourable William Harcourt   Earl Viscount and Baron Harcourt of
Stanton Harcourt, and Viscount Nuneham   of Nuneham Courtenay in the County of Oxford,
Master of the Horse to Her Most Excellent Majesty the Queen, General of His Majesty's Forces,
Colonel of the 16th Queen's Regiment of Light Dragoons (Lancers) Governor of Portsmouth
Lord Lieutenant of Windsor Forest, Deputy Ranger of Windsor Great Park &c &c &c 1818

APPENDIX. 103

HARCOURT[d] (on Dec. 13, 1776) was a great event at the time, as the former was looked upon by many as second only to Washington, and called the "Palladium of American liberty." Col. Harcourt was the son of Earl Harcourt, Lord Lieutenant of Ireland. A family connection existed between the Harcourts and the Evelyns of Wotton, Surrey; Elizabeth, the grand-daughter of John Evelyn (Author of "Sylva"), having in 1705 married the Hon. Simon Harcourt, son of Lord Chancellor Harcourt. Their daughter, Martha, was the sister of Simon, Earl Harcourt, and great-grandmother of Col. E. W. Harcourt, M.P., of Nuneham Park, the present head of the family. The Rev. William Evelyn, Vicar of Trim, Ireland, was private chaplain to Earl Harcourt, who, in 1775, had also made him Dean of Emley and Chancellor of Dromore, both ecclesiastical appointments in his gift.

It is stated that Col. Harcourt, before he left England, expressed hopes that he should take General Lee. He

[d] From the appearance of the following extract in the "New York Gazette," of Jan. 16, 1777, it would seem that it was suspected at the time that Lee had been treacherously betrayed; but it is now believed that the English account given above (which substantially agrees with Bancroft and Lossing) is the correct version of the way in which Lee's place of retreat was discovered by Col. Harcourt.

The "New York Gazette" of July 16, 1777, contains an account of the taking of General Lee, as published by order of Congress, the principal passages of which have been already mentioned, to which the following is added:—" Intelligence of General Lee's unguarded situation was given to the enemy the day before by an inhabitant of Baskenridge, personally known to the General, and who, under great professions of friendship for the American cause, was at heart the greatest deceiver that ever existed. This Judas rode all the preceding night to carry the intelligence, and served as a pilot to conduct the enemy, and came personally with them to the house where the General was taken."

arrived in New York in the first week in October, 1776[e], in the "Lapwing," which had several transports under convoy, having on board the 17th Regiment of Light Horse under his command.

Col. Harcourt (Dec. 13, 1776) was out on a reconnoitring expedition with about thirty Light Dragoons. He had passed the picket of the Provincials, of one hundred men, who did not turn out, supposing a larger body of the British troops near. He soon observed a man on foot going with great expedition, whom he imagined to be a spy, and had him secured. On searching him, a letter was found, the wafer not dry, directed to General Washington from General Lee. The man was informed if he did not immediately conduct them to the house where the gentleman was who gave him the letter, immediate death would be his lot. He complied, the house (which was about three miles from the Provincial army) was surrounded, and General Lee on hearing the firing, ran to the door with two French officers, one of whom, having exclaimed, "we are taken," raised his fusee to take aim at Col. Harcourt, which he observing, stooped his head, and the shot carried away the ribbon of his hair, wounding him slightly. The Frenchman was dispatched by the Dragoons. An officer, in a letter dated from New York, Dec. 21, 1776, states, that when Col. Harcourt approached the house[f] with his men, "they received

[e] About a month before the death of Capt. Evelyn, who was wounded Oct. 18, 1776, and carried to New York, where he died, Nov. 6, 1776.

[f] This statement differs from that of General James Wilkinson, who was in the house at the time. In his memoir, he says, that as the morning was cold, the guard had left their arms for a few moments, and were sunning themselves a little distance away. Col. Harcourt wrote to his father, that he captured Lee without the loss of a single man, and after some fire, retreated by another road.

GENERAL CHARLES LEE.

a fire from a guard that was in an outhouse, the two sentinels were killed, with several others (one account says seven or eight), without any loss on our side." Lee's behaviour was dastardly to the last. He got up into a corner, delivered his sword, and said he hoped his life was safe [g], and that it was terrible to be thus taken, when he had so many glorious schemes in hand. Col. Harcourt told him he would be well used. "By you, I may say (says Lee), but what am I to expect from the Howes?" General Lee was seized and led to the door, bareheaded; when he asked much to be allowed to go upstairs for his hat, but Col. Harcourt replied, "No, Mr. Lee, you can take a ride for once without your hat!" He was bound upon the horse of a guide, both legs and arms being well pinioned, and galloped off with such speed, that they went twenty miles in an hour and a quarter. "Only four minutes (Bancroft says) had elapsed, from the time of this surrounding of the house, before they started off on their return." Lee did not complain to the Colonel, but told him, for several miles he was not yet sure of his prey: but finding no rescue, which he expected as they passed almost through his out-parties, his spirits failed him, and he became sullen. For the first twenty-four hours he was defiant and (as English accounts say) insolent, and complained bitterly to Gen. Howe of the bad usage he met with. Gen. Howe replied by a card, which was addressed to him as Col. Lee, the rank which he held in the English army before his defection.

[g] "I do not know what lengths people may be disposed to proceed to on your side of the Atlantic; but in my own opinion, his life (Lee's), about which he is at least as anxious as one could imagine him, is effectually secured by the threats of retaliation."
Extract from a letter from Col. Harcourt, to his brother Lord Nuneham, dated 18th of March, 1777, from Brunswick.

He seemed much depressed after the receipt of this card[h]. He was taken eventually to Brunswick, and placed under a Captain's guard with two subalterns. He sent to Gen. Grant for money, but was refused, on the plea that he did not lack necessaries. He was very meanly dressed, and sent for a tailor to mend his clothes, "but not a man in the regiment," one of its officers writes, "would work for so great a rascal (as the gentlemen tailors called him)." The other Frenchman (Gayault), who had been with Lee only two days, as his aide-de-camp, and who, in endeavouring to escape into the woods, was captured, was to be one of their Colonels, but he had not yet received his commission. Col. Harcourt met a Yorkshireman who was acquainted with the country, and had him for a guide. He ordered the Frenchman to get up behind him, but he being not so alert as the Yorkshireman wished, he struck him on the head with his pistol, which so offended him, that he has not been in temper since; the indignity of being struck by a peasant is too mortifying for him, yet this fellow in his own country had not the rank of a gentleman. Another account states that Monsieur Gayault had been a Colonel in France. An English officer who had been acquainted with Gayault,

[h] The letter purporting to have been written by General Lee a few days after his capture, referred to by Mr. Bancroft, in vol. ix. p. 211, of his History of the U.S., had considerable publicity given to it in England. It appeared (amongst other papers) in the London "Morning Post and Daily Advertiser" of Feb. 19, 1777, but in the next issue was inserted the following:—"The letter laid before the publick as if written by General Lee to Capt. K———y is suspected to be an imposition, as by comparing it with a speech attributed to Caractacus when before Claudius, may more evidently appear." Two more letters were also published in the Dublin "Freeman's Journal" of the year 1777, as written by General Lee, both shewing very unmistakeably that they were fabrications.

APPENDIX. 107

says in a letter, "I saw Mr. Gayault, the Frenchman who was taken prisoner with Gen. Lee, at Brunswick, on his arrival with him. I provided him with quarters, where he was taken good care of, and supplied him with necessaries, and he was at liberty to walk about. Mr. Gayault informed me, that he was only two days with Gen. Lee, as aide-de-camp. That when he heard the firing of the Light Dragoons, he ran out hastily, and was taken prisoner."

When Gen. Lee was brought into the British camp, "he demanded to be received under the proclamation; but on being refused the benefit thereof, and told that he would be tried as a deserter[1], he flew into a most unbounded rage, and exclaimed against the repeated acts of false faith and treachery which had reduced him to his present situation."

A letter from New York to the writer's friend in Ireland, dated January 2, 1777, says:—"Yesterday, Gen. Lee and Col. Robert Livingstone were brought to town from the Jerseys, and confined in the old city hall. They were taken in the house of Captain Richards, (Bancroft and Lossing say at Mrs. White's inn at Baskingridge), about a mile from Trenton. I went this morning to the city hall to see my relation, poor Livingstone, but it made my heart ache to see him weep and lament. He said he would have made his peace agreeable to the commissioners' proclamation some time ago, but Gen. Lee

---

[1] Extract from a letter from New York, in the London "Morning Post" of March 5, 1777:—"Orders are gone for his trial (Lee's) by court-martial, of which General Matthews is to be president, for desertion. From which accusation, however, it is generally thought he will be acquitted; in which case he will be sent home, to be tried after the war is over, from which he will have very little hope of escape."

advised him to keep his hands clear of it, as it was only a trap to kidnap people." A paragraph in a newspaper of that period says, "that it is said that General Lee brooks his confinement very ill, and frequently behaves as if he was not in his perfect mind." Another account states that on the 20th of April, 1777,—"I find that General Lee is confined in a very decent room in the guard-house, contiguous to which is a small room in which he sleeps; is accompanied by the officers that are on guard over him, with whom he freely converses, but never on the subject of the disputes with the Colonies. He is allowed all necessaries that are requisite, and amongst others, a bottle of wine *per diem*. He is very careless in his apparel, and generally wears a brown short coat, or rather jacket." It was currently reported then that a "Lieutenant-General[k] (second in command to Lee), his aide-de-camp, an engineer and two sergeants, all Frenchmen, who were taken at the same time with Lee, were prisoners (Feb. 1777), on board the 'Inflexible' man-of-war, at the Nore."

After the capture of Lee, General Washington sent a formal message to General Howe demanding General Lee, and according to the terms of the cartel, offering Col. Campbell and three other Colonels (prisoners) for him. General Howe refused to exchange General Lee upon any terms, upon which General Washington ordered the four Colonels to be sent to prison.

Col. Harcourt having applied for leave of absence to return to England, it was intended that General Lee should have been taken over with him, if the current rumour is to be believed; and it is stated that he was

---

[k] Col. Harcourt says he was a French Lieutenant-Colonel.

SIMON EARL HARCOURT.

FATHER OF LIEUT. COLONEL WILLIAM HARCOURT,
AFTERWARDS FIELD MARSHALL EARL HARCOURT.

put upon board a vessel three several times in New York, in order to be brought to England, and the ship was absolutely (so the story runs) under sail, when Washington's second letter to General Howe arrived in New York, offering to exchange General Prescott for General Lee. His exchange was finally effected, and General Lee was released.

The capture of General Lee, when it was known in England, raised great hopes there of an early termination of the war. There was great rejoicing throughout the country[1], by those who sided with the Ministerial views of the necessity of coercion. "Upon Earl Harcourt's going to the King's levee (March 1, 1777), after the news of General Lee's being taken, the King came eagerly up to him,—'Oh! my lord, your son has behaved with the utmost gallantry; it gives me the utmost pleasure, and I doubt not it does the same to you,' which pleased his lordship not a little. His Majesty added, 'I shall take care of Colonel Harcourt; leave his fortune to me.'"

Earl Harcourt resigned his post in Ireland early in

---

[1] An example is here selected out of many others, to illustrate the manner by which, in one little village, it was proposed that the popular joy should be evinced.

The following advertisement was stuck in the market-place at Tring, in Hertfordshire, on Friday last :—

"*Feb.* 13, 1777.

"This is to give Notis that Thursday next will be helld as a day of regoicin in commemoration of the takin of General Lee, when their wil be a sermint preached, and other public demonstrascions of joye, after which will bee an nox roasted whole & everery mark of festivety & bell ringing imagenable, whith a ball & cock fiting at night in the hassembly room at the black Lyone.

"JAMES CLINCH,
"*Parish Clerk and Cryer.*"

1777, and retired to his seat at Nuneham Park. He was accidently drowned by falling into a well in his own park [m].

On more than one occasion during the war in America, Colonel Harcourt was indebted to the thoroughbred horse he rode for the preservation of his life. Once during the operations around Trenton, he was out on a scouting party, and suddenly came upon a strong force of Provincials. He put his horse at a high fence, but not being able to quite clear it, would have tumbled, had not the top rail, being a little decayed, given way, and let them over. A long distance was soon placed between the pursuers and the pursued, for Col. Harcourt's horse was remarkably fleet. This horse, it is said, lived to the extraordinary age of fifty years [n]. The late Mr. G. P. R.

---

[m] Sept. 16, 1777: "This day, at his seat at Nuneham, Oxfordshire, the body of Earl Harcourt was found dead in a narrow well in his park, with the head downwards, and nothing appearing above water but the feet and legs. It is imagined this melancholy accident was occasioned by his over-reaching himself in endeavouring to save the life of a favorite dog, who was found in the well with him, standing on his Lordship's feet. His hat and right-hand glove lay beside the well. Every possible method for the recovery of drowned persons was made use of for three several times, but unfortunately without effect."

[n] In a letter from Col. Harcourt to his father, dated 18th of June, 1777, from Brunswick, he says:—"Your little bay, high-mettled and shy as he is, at other times is perfectly quiet in fire, and is stout to a degree. The day I took General Lee, we marched near seventy miles, and he seemed as fresh the last moment as when I first mounted him." In a previous letter to his father, Earl Harcourt, he writes, May 31, 1777,—"I send you enclosed a copy of ——'s approbation of my conduct upon the occasion of my making General Lee a prisoner. Had I not lived quite so long about a Court, my vanity might have been gratified with the praises which have been lavished upon me; but when I recollect that the most eminent services of others have passed unrewarded, I cannot form great ex-

APPENDIX.

James, the novelist, who resided in Richmond, Virginia, as British Consul for several years, told a friend of Mr. B. J. Lossing's, in 1851, that he possessed a drawing of Col. Harcourt, and of the horse that he rode on the occasion of Lee's capture.

George III. was faithful to his promise of taking care of the future fortune of Col. Harcourt, who, on his return to England, was invested from time to time with honours, was frequently at court, and lived on terms of close intimacy with both the King and Queen. For the capture of Lee, he received the thanks of Parliament, which document is still in the possession of the present head of the family of Harcourt. In 1783 he was raised to the rank of Lieutenant-General, and in the following year had the command of part of the British forces in Holland. In 1809 he succeeded to his title on the death of his elder brother, and shortly after the coronation of George IV. was created a Field-Marshal.

Col. Harcourt fully merited all the rewards he received from his sovereign; for "he was a brave soldier, and was as staunch a supporter of government in the senate, as he had been in the field." He married in 1778, but left no issue, and the Harcourt property passed through a female line to the present possessor, Col. Edward Wil-

pectations from an event in which fortune had so considerable a share; with respect to rank, having failed in my wishes of obtaining it in the only manner that could have made it an object, I confess I am much better pleased with remaining in my present situation than if I had obtained a Brevet in a numerous promotion," and then he asks his father about the propriety of obtaining leave to return to England. His last letter to his father is dated 29th of November, 1777, from Philadelphia. He was present at the battle of Germantown, and engaged in the various operations around Philadelphia and in New Jersey, before his return to England.

liam Harcourt, M.P., of Nuneham Park, Abingdon, and of Stanton Harcourt, Oxon.

At an early period of his military career, General Lee, whilst stationed at Schenectady, had much intercourse with the Mohawk Indians, who surrounded that post, and who became so fond of him, that they adopted him into their tribe under the name of Ounewaterika, or Boiling-water. This soubriquet was particularly appropriate to Lee's character, for he was the very incarnation of feverish and restless energy. He was once in the service of the King of Portugal, and the following paragraph will shew the estimate formed of his character:—

"'Tis said that the King of Portugal left legacies to all the foreign officers as low as Colonels, who served with him during the war, except Col. Lee, (now in custody in New York); his restless and ambitious spirit was even then taken notice of, and rendered him despised."

The foregoing account of General Lee's capture[°] has been carefully compiled from the newspapers of that period, which contain numerous letters from officers and gentlemen at the seat of war and in New York, during the years 1776-8. Other reliable sources of information have also been drawn upon.

[°] An engraving from a private plate representing General Lee delivering up his sword to Col. William Harcourt, is at Nuneham, in the possession of Col. E. W. Harcourt. The engraver (Tomlinson) has made a mistake in the inscription on the plate in saying that Col. Harcourt had only fifteen men with him. He should have said thirty, as he informed his father by letter that he took that number with him on his expedition. He probably divided his force on his return, and took Lee to head quarters with fifteen men.

APPENDIX.

From "*Memoirs, &c., of General James Wilkinson,*" vol. i. pp. 101, 102.

Brigade-Major Wilkinson was dispatched on the morning of December 12, 1776, with a letter from General Gates to General Washington. At midnight he entered a wayside tavern, and roused up Col. George Gibson, and Joseph Nourse, Esq. (the Registrar of the Treasury), who directed him where to find General Lee, as they had parted from him the evening before. About 4 A.M. he reached Lee's quarters, at White's tavern, on Baskingridge.

"Wilkinson states that 'I was presented to the General as he lay in bed, and delivered into his hands the letter of General Gates. He examined the superscription, and observed it was addressed to General Washington, and declined opening it until I apprised him of the contents, and the motives of my visit. He then broke the seal and read it, after which he desired me to take repose. I lay down on my blanket before a comfortable fire, amidst the officers of his suite; for we were not in those days incumbered with beds or baggage. I arose at the dawn, but could not see the General, with whom I had been previously acquainted, before 8 o'clock. After some inquiries respecting the conduct of the campaign on the northern frontier, he gave me a brief account of the operations of the grand army, which he condemned in strong terms. He observed that our siege of Boston had led us into great errors; that the attempt to defend islands against a superior land and naval force was madness; that Sir William Howe could have given us checkmate at his discretion, and that we owed our salvation to his indolence, or disinclination to terminate the war. "When

APPENDIX.

I reached the army on York Island," said Lee, "all hands were busily employed in collecting materials, and erecting barracks; and I found little Mifflin exulting in the prospect of fine winter quarters at Kingsbridge. I replied to him, "Winter quarters here, Sir, and the British army still in the field! Go set fire to those you have built, and get away by the light, or Sir William Howe will find quarters for you."'

"General Lee wasted the morning in altercation with certain militia corps who were of his command, particularly the Connecticut Light Horse, several of whom appeared in large full-bottomed perukes, and were treated very irreverently. The call of the Adjutant-General for orders also occupied some of his time, and we did not sit down to breakfast before 10 o'clock. General Lee was engaged in answering General Gates' letter, and I had arisen from the table, and was looking out of an end window, down a lane about a hundred yards in length, which led to the house from the main road, when I discovered a party of British Dragoons turn a corner of the avenue at a full charge. Startled at the unexpected spectacle, I exclaimed, 'Here, Sir, are the British Cavalry.' 'Where?' replied the General, who had signed his letter on the instant. 'Around the house;' for they had opened files, and encompassed the building. General Lee appeared alarmed, yet collected; and his second observation marked his self-possession. 'Where is the guard? (d—n) the guard, why don't they fire?' And after a momentary pause, he turned to me and said, 'Sir, see what has become of the guard.' The women of the house at this moment entered the room, and proposed to him to conceal himself in a bed, which he rejected with evident disgust. I caught up my pistols which lay on the table, thrust the letter he had been writing into my pocket, and passed into a room at the opposite end of the house, where I had seen the guard in the morning. Here I discovered their arms; but the men were absent. I stepped out of the door, and perceived the Dragoons chasing them in different directions; and receiving a very uncivil salutation, I returned into the house.

"Too inexperienced immediately to penetrate the motives of this enterprise, I considered the rencontre accidental; and from terrific tales spread over the country of the violence and barbarity of the enemy, I believed it to be a wanton murdering party, and determined not to die without company. I accordingly sought a position where I could not be approached by more than one person at a time, and, with a pistol in each hand, I awaited the expected search, resolved to shoot the first and the second person who might appear, and then to appeal to my sword. I did not remain long in this unpleasant situation, but was apprised of the object of the incursion by the very audible declaration, 'If the General does not surrender in five minutes, I will set fire to the house,' which, after a short pause, was repeated with a solemn oath; and within two minutes I heard it proclaimed, 'Here is the General; he has surrendered.' A general shout ensued, the trumpet sounded the assembly, and the unfortunate Lee, mounted on my horse, which stood ready at the door, was hurried off in triumph, bare-headed, in his slippers and blanket-coat, his collar open, and his shirt very much soiled from several days' use.

"What a lesson of caution is to be derived from this event, and how important the admonition furnished by it! What an evidence of the caprice of fortune, of the fallibility of ambitious projects, and the inscrutable ways of Heaven! The capture of General Lee was felt as a public calamity; it cast a gloom over the country, and excited general sorrow. This sympathy was honourable to the people, and due to the stranger who had embarked his fortune with theirs, and determined to share their fate, under circumstances of more than common peril. Although this misfortune deprived the country of its most experienced chief, I have ever considered the deprivation a public blessing, ministered by the hand of Providence; for if General Lee had not abandoned caution for convenience, and taken quarters two miles from his army, on his exposed flank, he would have been safe; if a domestic traitor, who passed his quarters the same morning on private business, had not casually fallen in with Colonel Harcourt on a reconnoitring party, the General's quarters would not have been discovered; if my visit, and the controversy with the Connecticut Light Horse, had not spun out the morning unreasonably, the General would have been at his camp; if Colonel Harcourt had arrived an hour sooner, he would have found the guard under arms[p], and would have been repulsed, or resisted until succour could have arrived; if he had arrived half-an-hour later, the General would have been with his corps; if the guard had paid ordinary attention to their duty, and had not abandoned their arms, the General's quarters would have been defended; or if he had obeyed the peremptory and reiterated order of General Washington, he would have been beyond the reach of the enemy. And shall we impute to blind chance such a chain of rare incidents?

[p] The morning being cold, and the sun bright, they had left their station, crossed the main-road, and were sunning themselves on the south side of the house, about 200 yards from the tavern, which enabled Harcourt to cut them off from their arms.

I conscientiously reply in the negative, because the combination was too intricate and perplexed for accidental causes, or the agency of man; it must have been designed.

"General Lee merited severe punishment for his neglect of duty and disobedience of orders, and he received it from an unexpected hand. His offence was well understood by the army, and his misfortune was unpitied by those who reflected on the cause of it. It is a fact, he had very strong reasons for his neglect of General Washington's reiterated commands; but although they were not such as to justify the violation of a fundamental military principle, yet I verily believe his motives were patriotic, though intimately connected with a sinister ambition; for I am persuaded that, in the moment of his capture, he meditated a stroke against the enemy [q], which in its consequences would have depressed General Washington, elevated himself, and *immediately* served the cause of the United States. This opinion is supported by the following Letter to General Gates:—

"'*Baskingridge, Dec.* 13*th*, 1776.

"'MY DEAR GATES,—The ingenious manœuvre of Fort Washington has unhinged the goodly fabric we had been building. There never was so damned a stroke. *Entre nous* a certain great man is most damnably deficient. He has thrown me into a situation, where I have my choice of difficulties: if I stay in this province, I risk myself and army; and if I do not stay, the province is lost for ever. I have neither guides, cavalry, medicines, money, shoes, or stockings. I must act with the greatest circumspection.

[q] See Appendix, p. 105.

Tories are in my front, rear, and on my flanks; the mass of the people is strongly contaminated; in short, unless something, which I do not expect, turns up, we are lost; our counsels have been weak to the last degree. As to what relates to yourself; if you think you can be in time to aid the General, I would have you by all means go; you will, at least, save your army. It is said that the Whigs are determined to set fire to Philadelphia; if they strike this decisive stroke, the day will be our own; but unless it is done, all chance of liberty in any part of the globe is for ever vanished. Adieu, my dear friend! God bless you!

"'CHARLES LEE.'

"So soon as Lieut.-Col. Harcourt retreated with his prize, I repaired to the stable, mounted the first horse I could find, and rode full speed to General Sullivan, whom I found under march towards Pluckamin. I had not examined General Lee's letter; but believing a knowledge of the contents might be useful to General Sullivan, who succeeded him in command, I handed it to him; who after the perusal returned it, with his thanks, and advised me to rejoin General Gates without delay, which I did the next morning, at Sussex Court-house, whither he had led the troops from Van Kempt's.

"Lee's misfortune afflicted Gates profoundly; they had been long acquainted, had served together in the British army, and were personally attached; their politics and political connexions were in unison, and their sympathies and antipathies ran in the same current: yet long after, and in misfortune, they became estranged."

APPENDIX. 119

EDWARD THOROTON GOULD[r] was the son of Edward Gould, Esq., of Mansfield Woodhouse, in the county of Nottinghamshire, by Mary his wife, daughter of Robert Thoroton, of Screveton Hall, (who was descended from a younger brother of the Nottinghamshire historian of that name).

He was commissioned to the 4th Foot as ensign, on the 20th of February, 1767; promoted to be lieutenant on the 14th of November, 1771; sold out on the 26th of January, 1776. He was wounded and taken prisoner at Concord, and was afterwards exchanged, and returned to England. Just six days after his capture, he made an affidavit (herewith appended) at Medford, Massachusetts (in relation to the skirmish at Concord), which document was duly attested before three justices of the peace. This affidavit he was, no doubt, persuaded to draw up and sign, and send to Mr. Woodfall, the editor of the famous paper called "The Public Advertiser," the same journal in which originally appeared the "Letters of Junius." Lieut. Gould was also subpœnaed to appear as a witness at the trial of the Rev. John Horne, where he gave a *viva voce* account of the battles of Lexington and Concord, and adhered to all the statements in his affidavit, much to the annoyance of George III. and his Ministers.

In 1781 he was appointed Lieut.-Col. of the old 42nd (or Nottinghamshire) regiment of militia, and became Colonel of that regiment in 1791, upon the resignation of the Hon. Henry Willoughby (afterwards Lord Middleton). He served with this regiment for some years, volunteering for service in Spain in 1808; he left the service in 1819. He was for many years a justice of the peace for Nottinghamshire, and served as High Sheriff in 1792;

---

[r] "Poor Little Gould," p. 55.

which latter fact is a little remarkable, as he was exempt from this office as a military officer. He married, first, the Lady Barbara Yelverton, only daughter and heiress of Henry, third Earl of Sussex, fourth Viscount Langueville, and eighteenth Baron Grey de Ruthyn; by this lady (with whom he eloped) he had one son and two daughters. His second wife (to whom he was married in 1791) was the Hon. Anne Dormer, eldest daughter of Charles, eighth Lord Dormer. After he left the service, he resided abroad, and died in Paris at the Hôtel Breteuil, on the 15th of February, 1830, and was buried in Père la Chaise. His son, Henry, succeeded to the Barony of Grey de Ruthyn, upon the death of his grandfather in 1799, and assumed the name and arms of Yelverton. He was (like his father) a wild and dissipated man; and having run away with a Warwickshire farmer's daughter named Kelham, he was pursued by her brother, and compelled to marry her, and by her he was the father of the late Lady Grey de Ruthyn.

In a letter from the Hon. Mrs. Boscawen to Mrs. Delany, dated Nov. 1, 1775, she writes:—" Have you not pitied poor Lady Sussex, my dear Madam? She has been often at this village (Colney Hatch), with her sister (Mrs. Durell), of whom I have enquired after her health, and have had a very bad account, her agonies having been very great. My lord has made a will, which cuts off this ungrateful child with a shilling, but it is to be hoped he will live to cancel it and forgive her; but it must be a very bad child, I should fear, that can plant a dagger in her parents' breasts, in return for all their care and tenderness: *such a child too!* The boldness amazes me. She was sixteen last June. Lieut. Gould, her husband, is the same young man who was wounded and taken prisoner in ye first action with the Americans; he came over after ye 2nd (being exchanged), and came to me at my son's desire, to bring his letters and assure me of his safety, he and my boy being in the same regiment. Gould is not a soldier of fortune, but has a small estate in Nottinghamshire in possession, his father being lately dead. One of his sisters is marryd to Lady Sussex's brother, from whence I suppose this unhappy connection arose."—From *Life and Letters of Mary Granville (Mrs. Delany)*, vol. ii.

"*The Public Advertiser*," May 31st, 1775.

"For the 'Public Advertiser,' Authentic Copy, Lexington, 25 April, 1775.

"I, Edward Thoroton Gould, of his Majesty's Own Regiment of Foot, being of lawful age, do testify and declare, that on the evening of the 18th inst., under the orders of General Gage, I embarked with the Light Infantry and Grenadiers of the line, commanded by Col. Smith, and landed on the marshes of Cambridge, from whence we proceeded to Lexington.

"On our arrival at that place we saw a body of Provincial troops armed, to the number of about 60 or 70 men. On our approach they dispersed, and soon after firing began; but which party fired first I cannot exactly say, as our troops rushed on shouting and huzzaing previous to the firing, which was continued by our troops so long as any of the Provincials were to be seen. From thence we marched to Concord. On a hill near the entrance of the town we saw another body of Provincials assembled. The Light Infantry companies were ordered up the hill to disperse them. On our approach they retreated towards Concord. The Grenadiers continued the road under the hill towards the town. Six companies of the Light Infantry were ordered down to take possession of the bridge which the Provincials retreated over; the company I commanded was one. Three companies of the above detachment went forwards about two miles. In the meantime the Provincial troops returned, to the number of about three or four hundred. We drew up on the Concord side of the bridge. The Provincials came down upon us, upon which we engaged, and gave the first fire. This was the first engagement after the one at Lexington; a continued firing from both parties lasted through the whole day. I myself was wounded at the attack of the bridge, and am now treated with the greatest humanity, and taken all possible care of, by the Provincials at Medford.

<p style="text-align:center">"EDW. THOROTON GOULD,
"<i>Lieutenant of the King's Own Regiment.</i></p>

"*Medford, April* 25, 1775.

<p style="text-align:center">"Province of the Massachusetts Bay, Middlesex County,
"<i>April</i> 25, 1775.</p>

"LIEUTENANT EDWARD THOROTON GOULD, above named, personally made oath to the truth of the foregoing Declaration by him subscribed, and wrote with his own hands.

<p style="text-align:center">" Before us,
"THAD. MASON,
"JOSIAH JOHNSON,
"SIMON TUFTS,
"<i>Justices of the Peace for the County
aforesaid. Quorum unis.</i>"</p>

From "*Public Advertiser,*" *Dec.* 13, 1776.

"Yesterday morning, precisely at 9 o'clock, came on in Guildhall, before Lord Mansfield and a special jury, the trial of the printers of the London 'Evening Post,' on an information filed against them by the Attorney-General, for printing and publishing, so far back as 1775, the following advertisement :—

"'*King's Arms Tavern, Cornhill,*
"'*June* 7, 1775.

"'At a special meeting this day, several members of the Constitutional Society, during an adjournment,

"'A gentleman proposed that a subscription should be immediately entered into (by such of the Members present who might approve the purpose) for raising the sum of £100, "to be applied to the relief of the widows, orphans, and aged parents of our beloved American subjects, who, faithful to the character of Englishmen, preferring death to slavery, were, for that reason only, inhumanly murdered by the King's troops, at or near Lexington and Concord, in the province of Massachusetts, on the 19th of April last."

"'Which sum being immediately collected, it was therefore resolved,

"'That Mr. Horne do pay to-morrow into the hands of Messrs. Brownes and Collinson, on the account of Dr. Franklin, the said sum of £100, and that Dr. Franklin be requested to apply the same to the above-mentioned purpose.

"'JOHN HORNE.'"

APPENDIX.

Mr. Horne afterwards assumed the name of Tooke, to inherit some £8,000 of a gentleman of that name, of Purley, in Surrey, and wrote the work called "Diversions of Purley."

The printers were found guilty in five minutes after the jury withdrew. Mr. Horne's trial came on July 4, 1777, before Lord Mansfield, Mr. John Wilkes, Edmund Burke, and Lord Percy sitting on the bench as spectators. Horne desired the crier to summon Lord George Germaine and General Gage as witnesses, but they did not appear.

"Lieut. Edward Thoroton Gould was examined respecting an affidavit made by him about the affair at Lexington, and published in one of the 'Public Advertisers,' produced by the defendant. He acknowledged it to be his affidavit, and swore to the contents, giving at the same time a *viva voce* account of the action ; whereby it clearly appears that the rebels were armed, ready to receive the King's troops, and that the latter heard the alarm-guns firing whilst they were on the march."

Mr. Horne was found guilty Sept., 1777, and received his sentence Nov. 23, 1777. He was sentenced to pay a fine of £200, and to be imprisoned for twelve months ; and afterwards to find surety for himself in £400, and two sureties of £200 each, for good behaviour for two years.

Another of his productions was called "Glencoe," in which he insinuated that the battle of Lexington was another "Massacre of Glencoe." During the trial he pleaded his own cause with the greatest ability, tact, and legal knowledge. In 1771 he had a literary duel with the celebrated "Junius," and the general opinion at the time was, that he was victor in the contest.

After the trial, it was stated "that Mr. Horne's examining of Mr. Gould was very injudicious, for by his evidence it appeared that, as soon as the troops began to march, alarm-guns were fired by the rebels, who thereupon assembled and formed, and soon began to fire random shots upon our men. Before Mr. Gould gave his testimony, many present believed that our troops had murdered the natives sleeping in their houses, and that it would be proved by Mr. Gould's evidence."

From "London Chronicle," May 30, to June 1, 1775.

The following affidavits and other particulars, relative to the late skirmish between His Majesty's troops and the Provincials in Massachusetts bay, were received on Monday last:—

"*April* 23, 1775, *Lincoln.*—I, John Bateman, belonging to the 52nd Regiment, commanded by Col. Jones, on Wednesday morning, on the 19th of April instant, was in the party marching for Concord, being at Lexington, in the county of Middlesex; being nigh the meeting-house in said Lexington, there was a small party of men gathered together in that place, when our said troops marched by, and I testify and declare that I heard the word of command given to the troops to fire, and some of the said troops did fire; and I saw one of the said small party lie dead on the ground, nigh the said meeting-house; and I testify, that I never heard any of the inhabitants so much as fire one gun on the said troops."

"Sworn before John Cuming and Duncan Ingraham, Justices of the Peace."

"*Concord, April* 23, 1776.—I, James Marr, of lawful age, testify and say that, in the evening of the 18th instant, I received orders from George Hutchinson, Adjutant of the 4th Regiment of regular troops stationed at Boston, to prepare and march; to which orders I attended, and marched to Concord, where I was ordered by an officer, with about one hundred men, to guard a certain bridge there; while attending that service, a number of people came along, in order, as I suppose, to cross the said bridge, at which time a number of the regular troops first fired upon them."

"Sworn before Duncan Ingraham, and Jonas Dix, Justices of the Peace."

HUGH, EARL PERCY[s], born Aug. 14, 1742, returned to England after the war, and became second Duke of Northumberland on the death of his father in 1786. He died 10th of July, 1817. He was at the battle of Lexington, where he brought off the exhausted troops, who had been defeated through the mismanagement of the officer (Smith) in command. He was grand-uncle to the present distinguished Lord Privy Seal, Algernon George, sixth Duke of Northumberland. Earl Percy was an excellent officer, and was possessed of a generous, humane and benevolent nature. The various letter-writers from the seat of war testify to his ability in the field, and his great popularity in the service, and are lavish of their praises of him for his many acts of humanity and generosity. Here is one example from the "London Chronicle" for Sept. 7—10, 1776:—"A soldier lately returned from America, having seen in the paper an account of the respect shewn by

[s] "Lord Percy," p. 44.

Earl Percy. 1775.

the magistrates of Westminster to their excellent representative, Lord Percy, desires us to communicate a few out of the many instances of his humanity and generosity.

"After the fatal attack at Bunker's Hill, his lordship gave to the widow of every soldier of his regiment, who fell in that action, an immediate benefaction of seven dollars; he paid their passage home, and ordered five guineas to be distributed to each of them on their landing in Britain. His humanity to the sick and wounded (sending them wine, fresh provisions, &c.), and his generosity to their families during their long stay at Boston, have been mentioned. Perhaps the following particulars deserve notice. He had a large tent provided for every company at his own expense to accommodate their women, and he makes it a rule to receive no other servants into his family but soldiers or their wives. Though his regiment is distinguished for its admirable discipline, he never will suffer the private men to be struck, or used in a manner unbecoming Englishmen and soldiers; but endeavours to win them to their duty by generous treatment, by rewards, and his own excellent example, so that he is perfectly adored among them: requiring no service from the meanest sentinel, which he is not ready to share with them, whether as to hardship, fatigue or danger. He is equally beloved and respected by his officers, among whom he lives with all the equality of a brother, yet always exerting a manly firmness in whatever relates to command or duty. His fortune he considers only as a bank to assist merit, that is unprotected and unfriended. And notwithstanding the delicate and concealed manner in which this young nobleman dispenses his favours, this informant has known no fewer than seven instances in which his lordship has purchased commissions for excellent men and good officers, who must have seen their juniors rise over their heads, while they had languished in neglect and obscurity. One of these commissions is well known to have cost him more than nine hundred pounds."

"'London Chronicle,' June 10—13, 1775:—We hear that all the letters from Boston mention that Lord Percy has acquired great honour by his spirit and conduct, that he was in every place of danger, cool and deliberate, and wise in all his orders; and though continually in a shower of bullets, and an object that was aimed at, as he was on horseback, yet that he happily came off unhurt." Yet he seems to have had several narrow escapes, as the following will shew:—"We are assured that Lord Percy, in the late skirmish (Lexington) with the Americans, had a narrow escape for his life; a musket-ball, which it is supposed came transversely, having struck one of the middle buttons of his waistcoat, and from thence passed off slanting, so as to leave only a mark behind." "A letter from a gentleman in the army at N.Y., to his father in Alnwick, confirms the accounts of Lord Percy's horse having been shot under him at the siege of Fort Washington."

"May 3, 1777, London.—A ship is arrived at Liverpool which sailed from New York the 23rd of March. Nothing material had then happened between the armies, but it is whispered that Earl Percy has desired leave to come home, and that Sir William Howe has also desired that his Lordship should be recalled. The occasion of the misunderstanding between them is said to proceed from a disobedience of orders. When the winter quarters of Lord Cornwallis were beat up, and the Hessians surprised at Trenton, General Howe ordered Earl Percy to send back 2,000 men (another account says 1,500) of the troops in Rhode Island. His lordship thought that it would weaken his garrison too much, therefore he only sent 1,000 men. This has occasioned altercation and mutual complaints, and made it impossible for the generals to serve together."

A strenuous denial of the truth of the above statement appeared in the London Journals, instigated, no doubt, by the Government. Yet the frequency with which this want of unity between the two officers is alluded to by succeeding letter-writers, would warrant a belief that there was much truth in the common report. Another writer states that "Lord Percy placed the matter in the hands of his father, who repaired to George the Third, and asked leave for the recall of his son. The king was much embarrassed at this proposal, yet granted his request."

"New York, March 14, 1777.— On General Clinton's return to take the command of the troops at Rhode Island, it is understood that Lord Percy will desire leave to return home. Should that take place, his absence will be sincerely regretted by every person now serving under his lordship, from the second in command to the private sentinel."

"May 20, 1777.—Letters received from America speak in very strong terms of the disagreeable situation which Lord Percy has been in at Rhode Island. It is well known his lordship was to have been sent thither on a separate command with eight or ten thousand men; but when this plan was carried into execution, they fell considerably short of those numbers, and they have been so much lessened since by draughts made from thence, in order to repair the losses occasioned by the late misconduct in the Jerseys, that Lord Percy, instead of having it in his power to display his courage and military skill by attacks on the enemy, has scarce had sufficient force remaining to protect himself from insult."

"'Public Advertiser,' June 7, 1777.—On Monday last arrived at Falmouth, in the 'Mercury' packet, after a passage of twenty-eight days, the Right Hon. Earl Percy, Lieutenant-General in America, where his lordship has been employed in the service of his country from the very beginning of the American war, and by his distinguished spirit and military skill, as well as by his generosity and humanity to the soldiers, has gained universal esteem and admiration. His absence, it is to be feared, will be felt and lamented by the whole army, and it will be much to be regretted if any event has happened that should have forced him to withdraw from a service which he had pursued with so much ardour and success; but history affords too many instances how much exalted merit is exposed to jealousy and envy."

Before leaving Newport on May 3, 1777, a long address was presented to Lord Percy by the loyal inhabitants of the town, on his return to England. Under date of Dec. 3, 1776, a Lieutenant-Colonel in the army placed the following postscript to a letter:—"P.S. Little Percy has behaved like an angel; he remains with us, notwithstanding he had the King's leave to return to Europe five months ago."

"June 10-12th, 1777: London.—When Lord Percy quitted Rhode Island, there was a general lamentation among the people. This may be relied on. Nor was it ever distinguishable whether his Lordship's zeal for his country, or his feelings for the distressed, had the greater influence on his mind, except when an object actually presented itself, and then all the tenderness of a Christian prevailed over every sentiment; though the esteem and duty of a soldier were still unshaken and inviolate in his generous breast."

Extract from a letter from Portsmouth, (June 6th):— "The Earl Percy, upon his arrival in London, waited upon Lord George Germaine, who immediately ordered his postchaise, and took him to Kew, where he was most graciously received, and had an audience with his Majesty near two hours." "The arrival of Earl Percy from America has much embarrassed the Administration, who are fully convinced that the loss of such an able and enterprizing officer, at this crisis, may prove very fatal to their measures."

June 10-12, 1777:—"It is said that Earl Percy will return to America with a commission of importance, and will embark for that purpose on board a frigate, which is to sail for New York the middle of next month."

June 24, 1777:—"We are assured that though it has been suggested to the Lord Percy, by desire of a great personage, that after so much fatiguing service as he has gone through his further services would be readily dispensed with, yet that gallant young nobleman is so wedded to the business, that he is determined not to return till it is completed."

The Hon. Mrs. Boscawen[†].

From Boswell's "Life of Johnson," p. 608:—"On Wednesday, April 29, (1778), I dined with him (Johnson) at Mr. Allen Ramsey's, where were Lord Binning, Dr. Robert-

[†] Page 83.

son the historian, Sir Joshua Reynolds, and the Hon. Mrs. Boscawen, widow of the Admiral, and mother of the present Viscount Falmouth, of whom, if it be not presumptuous in me to praise her, I would say that her manners are the most agreeable, and her conversation the best, of any lady with whom I ever had the happiness to be acquainted."

On p. 646 will be found a letter from Bennett Langton to Boswell, in which he writes, that one evening he was at Mr. Vesey's, where the company consisted chiefly of ladies, among whom "the Duchess of Beaufort must, I suppose, from her rank be named before her mother, Mrs. Boscawen, and her elder sister, Mrs. Lewson, who was likewise there." Croker, the editor of Johnson's life, adds in a note, that "Mrs. Boscawen and her daughters, Mrs. Leveson (pronounced Lewson) Gower and the Dutchess of Beaufort, are celebrated in Miss Hannah More's Poem, entitled 'Sensibility:'—

'All Leveson's sweetness and all Beaufort's grace.'"

On Friday, April 20, (1781,) Boswell says,—"I spent with him (Johnson) one of the happiest days that I remember to have enjoyed in the whole course of my life," at Mrs. Garrick's, in London, at her house in the Adelphi. "The company was Miss Hannah More, who lived with her, and whom she called her chaplain, Mrs. Boscawen, Mrs. Elizabeth Carter, Sir Joshua Reynolds, Dr. Burney, Dr. Johnson, and myself. We were all in fine spirits, and I whispered to Mrs. Boscawen, 'I believe this is as much as can be made of life.'" To which remark Croker appends a note that "Boswell was right; four other such women or such men it would have been difficult to collect. Mrs. Boscawen shone with her usual mild lustre." During the evening Dr. Johnson said, "I love 'Blair's Sermons. Though the dog is a Scotchman and a presbyterian, and everything he should not be, I was the first to praise them. Such was my candour (smiling)." *Mrs. Boscawen.*—"Such his great merit, to get the better of all your prejudices." *Johnson.*—"Why, Madam, let us compound the matter; let us ascribe it to my candour and his merit." At one time, Mrs. Boscawen owned and lived in the villa once occupied by the poet Thompson at Kew-lane, Richmond, and which was called by her "Rosedale." She greatly extended the pleasure-grounds, which were in the poet's time narrow in extent. She religiously preserved the reliques of an alcove which formed the summer study of the poet. She died in South Audley Street, London, March 26, 1805, aged 86 years.

List of Officers serving in 4th Foot in 1774.

COLONEL.   Lt.-General Studholme Hodgson.
LT.-COL.   George Maddison. *Present.*
MAJORS.   James Boorder. *Retired* 23. 4. 1774.
           James Ogilvie. *Present.*
CAPTAINS. John Webster. *Present.*
           Nisbitt Balfour. *Present.*
           Thomas Thomlinson. *Present.*
           John West. *Present.*
           William Holmes.
           W. Glanville Evelyn. *Present. Killed* 1775, (*sic*)[u].
           Charles Cochrane. *Present.*
CAPT.-LIEUT. John Farrier. *Present.*

[u] Capt. W. G. Evelyn was wounded Oct. 18, 1776; and died in New York, Nov. 6, 1776.

APPENDIX.

LIEUTENANTS. Joseph Knight.
John Crammond.
George Hutchinson, (Adjt.). *Present.*
Harry Rooke.
Edward Barron. *Present.*
Leonard Browne. *Present.*
Benjamin Fish. *Present.*
Peregrine Fra. Thorne. *Present.*
Edward Gould.
John Barker. *Present.*
David Hamilton. *Present.*

ENSIGNS. Henry Hyatt.
James Goddard Butler. *Present.*
Thomas Russell. *Present.*
Christopher Breary. *Present.*
John Hay. *Present.*
John Thomas Maddison. *Present.*
Forbes Champagné. *Present.*
David Campbell.

CHAPLAIN. James Burch. *Present.*

ADJUTANT. George Hutchinson. *Present.*

QUARTERMASTER. Harry Rooke.

SURGEON. Richard Knowles. *Present.*

The 4th Foot embarked for North America on April 17, 1774. The officers shewn as present in the above list are those so reported in the Muster Rolls of the Regiment, at the time of embarkation.

It will be observed that the name of Ensign George Evelyn Boscawen is missing; as he sailed later, in the ship-of-war commanded by his brother-in-law, Admiral John Leveson Gower, who promised, in one of his letters to Mrs. Boscawen, "to look after him as if he was his own son."

Table of Descent to Illustrate Captain Evelyn's Letters.

George Evelyn, of Nutfield, Surrey, M.P. for Bletchingley, died 1699; great grandson of George Evelyn, Esq., of Wotton, who died in 1603. He married = **For his third wife, Frances, daughter of Andrew Bromhall, Esq., of Stoke Newington, co. Middlesex. Was descended from an ancient Bedfordshire family.**

Richard Evelyn, born 1685, died at Dublin in 1751. = **Jane Meade,** sister to Alderman Thomas Meade, Lord Mayor of Dublin,.. 1758.

Wm. Evelyn Glanville, changed his name to Glanville on his marriage. = **Frances,** dau. and heiress of William Glanville, Esquire.

William Evelyn, Rector of Trim, and afterwards Dean of Emley, in Ireland, died at Dublin, March 28, 1777: born in 1718. = **Margaret,** daughter of Christopher Chamberlain, Esquire, of Chamberlainstown, co. Meath, Ireland, died at Dublin in 1789.

Frances Evelyn, only child, married in 1742 to = **The Hon. Edward Boscawen,** Admiral of the Blue, R.N., died Jan. 10, 1761: born in 1711.

Wm. Glanville Evelyn, eldest son; born at Arklow, co. Wicklow, Ireland, in 1742; died at New York, U. S., Nov. 6, 1776.

John Evelyn, second son, heir to his brother William; born at Arklow, co. Wicklow, Ireland, June 1, 1743; died at Wotton, Surrey, Nov. 27, 1827. He was the grandfather of the present (1879) head of the Evelyn family, W. J. Evelyn, Esq., of Wotton House, Surrey.

George Evelyn, youngest son; buried at Portglinone, Ireland, in 1756.

Edward Hugh, eldest son; born Sept. 13, 1744; died at "Spa," Germany, July 17, 1774; M.P. for Truro; buried at St. Michael's, Penkivel, Cornwall.

Wm. Glanville Boscawen, second son, died in the Island of Jamaica, April 21, 1769, a lieutenant in the British Navy.

George Evelyn Boscawen, third son, became third Lord Falmouth; born May 6, 1758; died Feb. 1808; buried at St. Michael's, Penkivel, Cornwall.

Frances, married Admiral the Hon. John Leveson-Gower, brother to first Marquis of Stafford.

Elizabeth Boscawen, married Henry, fifth Duke of Beaufort.

INDEX.

ADAMS, John, his autobiography of Samuel Adams quoted, 47; assumed the name of Novanglus, 49.
—— Samuel, father of the Governor, 47.
—— Samuel, ordered to be seized, 8; testimony of his abilities, 46; genealogical note, 47.
Allen, Col. Ethan, inhuman treatment of, 101, 102.
Amherst, Gen. Jeffery, declines the command in America, 80.
Arklow, Ireland, 6.
Auchmuty, Miss, 35.

Badminton, Gloucestershire, 88.
Balfour, Nisbitt, Capt. 4th Foot, 70, 133; biographical note, 83.
Barker, John, Lieut. 4th Foot, 134.
Barron, Edward, Lieut. 4th Foot, 134.
Baskenridge, ——., accused of having betrayed General Lee, 103.
Bateman, John, his affidavit concerning the Battles of Lexington and Concord, 125.
Beaufort, Henry, fifth Duke of, 135.
Belvedere, America, 18.
Binning, Lord, 131.
Bishop, Major, returns to England, 65.
Blair's Sermons, praised by Johnson, 133.
Bland, Humphrey, author of "Military Discipline," 31.
Bletchingley, Surrey, 3, 5, 135.
Boorder, James, Major, 4th Regiment, 133.
Boscawen, Edward, Admiral of the blue, 30, 135; biographical note, 87.
—— Elizabeth, wife of Henry, fifth Duke of Beaufort, 132, 135.
—— Frances, letter to her, 83; letter from her (extract), 120; notes concerning her, from Boswell's "Life of Johnson," 131—133.

Boscawen, George Evelyn, 8, 134; genealogical notes, 29—31; created Viscount Falmouth, 30; his exemplary conduct, 32, 33; appointed Lieut. 63rd Foot, 73.
—— Hugh, note of his death, 31.
Boston, America, 8, 9, 51, 113.
Boswell, James, extracts from his "Life of Johnson," 131—133.
Breary, Christopher, Ensign, 4th Foot, 134.
Brown, Sir Richard, 1.
Browne. Leonard, Lieut. 4th Foot, 134.
Bruce, Edward le, 6.
Bunker's Hill, battle of, 9, 61, 62.
Burch, James, Chaplain 4th Foot, 134.
Burgoyne, General, 66; his character, 74; author of the farce, "Blockade of Boston," 80.
Burke, Edmund, present at Horne Tooke's trial, 124.
Burney, Dr., 132.
Bushers, Mr., in Bedford-street, 43.
Butler, James Goddard, Ensign, 4th Foot, 134.

Cadwallader, Dr., to report concerning the health of Gen. Prescott, 101, 102.
Calvert, Leonard, 24.
Campbell, David, Ensign, 4th Foot, 134.
Canada, 34.
Carolina, America, 81.
Carter, Mrs. Elizabeth, 132.
Chadets, Capt., 30.
Chamberlain, Christopher, 6.
—— Tankerville, 6.
Champagné, Forbes, Ensign, 4th Foot, 41, 134.
Charlestown, America, 71.
Chatham, Lord, opinion of Admiral Boscawen, 87.
Cleaveland, Col., 35; commands the Royal Artillery, 98; distinguishes himself, 99.

INDEX.

Clinch, James, parish clerk of Tring, 109.
Cochrane, Charles, Capt. 4th Foot, 133.
Colthurst, Lieut., killed, 63.
Comber, William, 22.
Concord, America, 8; battle there, 54—57, 119.
Crammond, John, Lieut. 4th Foot, 134.
Crane, Jane, wife of George Evelyn, 25.
—— Richard, 25.
Cuming, John, 125.

Dana, Elizabeth Ellery, journal possessed by her quoted, 59.
Deverson, Capt., 43.
Disraeli, Benjamin, quotation from "Lothair" concerning John Evelyn, 2.
Dix, Jonas, 126.
Dormer, —., wife of Edward T. Gould, 120.
Dowdall, Wat., 67.
Dromore, 58.
Dunmore, Lord, 81.
Dymoke, Mr., 44.

Elizabeth, Queen, grants a patent to John and Robert Evelyn, 20.
Emley, Ireland, 1.
Evelyn, family of, settled at Long Ditton, Godstone, and Wotton, 1; family of, at Nutfield, pedigree, 135; family portraits at Wotton, 6.
—— Anna, wife of Henry Haines, 25.
—— Catharine, wife of Thomas Stoughton, 22.
—— Charles, 25.
—— Elizabeth, wife of Anthony Gamage, 25.
—— Frances, wife of Edward Boscawen, 135.
—————— wife of Harry Kelsey, 25.
—— Frederick, Bart., 12.
—— George, died 1603, 1, 135.
—————— Capt., appointed commander of the Isle of Kent, Maryland, 24.
—————— of Nutfield, mention of him in Evelyn's Diary, 4, 5, 135.
—————— M.P. for Bletchingley, 5; dies suddenly, 5; portrait of him at Wotton, 6.

Evelyn, George, of Wotton, monument, 20.
—— James, 12, 25.
—— Jane, wife of —. Freemans, 25.
—— Joan, letter to her, 23, 24.
—— John, author of "Sylva," biographical note, 1, 2; quotations from his Diary, 2—6; manuscript of his Diary now preserved at Wotton, 2; buried at Wotton, 2.
—— Sir John, of Godstone, mentioned in Evelyn's Diary, 2—4; M.P. for Bletchingley, 3; portrait at Wotton, 6.
—— John, son of John, of Say's Court, note of his birth and christening, 3, 4.
—— Sir John, of Wilts, M.P. for Ludgershall, 3; declared a traitor, ib.
—— Margaret, mother of W. G. E., 135; letter to her, 88.
—————— wife of John Knatchbull, 25.
—— Mary, 25.
—— Mountjoy, 25.
—— Rebecca, 25.
—— Richard, of Wotton, 1, 20.
—————— grandfather of W. G. E., 5.
—— Robert, Memoir, 15—24; emigrates to Virginia, 15; his description of the province of New Albion, 19; fragment of a letter to his step-mother, 23, 24; descent from him, 25.
—— Rose, 25.
—— Thomas, 20.
—— William, Dean of Emley, and Vicar of Trim, 1, 103; letters to, 26, 38, 45, 53, 66, 68, 71, 81, 95.
—— William Glanville, 133, 135; memoir, 1—14; obtains an ensigncy, 6; embarks for Boston, 8; mentioned in Gen. Howe's despatch, 10; dies from his wounds, 11; his character, ib.; description of his voyage and arrival at Boston, 27; his opinion of the Americans, 28, 51; eulogizes the exemplary conduct of his friend, Ensign Boscawen, 32, 33; describes the progress of the rebellion in America, 34—36, 38—40, 48, 49; his opinion of Col. Prescott, 42; note of

the influence of Samuel Adams, 46; describes the battle of Concord, 53—55; his remarks upon his father's preferment, 58; anxiety on account of Ensign Boscawen, 59, 60; recounts the successes of the rebels, 63, 64; and the difficulties and impediments in subduing them, 64, 65; advises extermination, 65; account of a surprise and failure of the Fleet, 68; suggests means to his father by which he may gain advancement, 69, 70; scarcity and price of fresh provisions, 72; English flag daily insulted by cruisers, 72; capture of an English brig, 72, 73; noticed by his General, and employed in reconnoitring, 74, 78; is thanked for his services, 75; accompanies Gen. Clinton on an expedition, 78; describes an alarm during a performance at the theatre, 79; details of the gaining of New York, 83—85, 89; captures five American officers, 89; copy of his will, 90; statement of his effects, 92; sends particulars of a victory over the French in the Seven Years' War, 96.

Evelyn, William Glanville, Letters to his father, 26, 38, 45, 53, 66, 68, 71, 81, 95; to his mother, 88; to Mrs. Leveson Gower, 29, 31, 41, 58, 63, 76; to Mrs. Boscawen, 83.

Farrier, John, Capt.-Lieut. 4th Regiment, 133.
Felbridge, Surrey, 12.
Fish, Benjamin, Lieut. 4th Foot, 134.
Fontainebleau, treaty of, 7.
Franklin, Benjamin, 123.

Gage, Gen., lands at Boston, 8; his action in dissolving the Boston Council, 28.
Galloway, Joseph, 94.
Gamage, Anthony, 25.
Garrick, Mrs., 133.
Gates, Gen., 113; letter from Gen. Lee, 117.
Gayault, Monsieur, taken prisoner, 106.
George III., King, rewards Col. Harcourt, 111.

Germaine, Lord George, 9, 124.
Germantown, Battle of, 41.
Gerrard, Lady, 4.
Gibson, Col. George, 113.
Glanville, Frances Evelyn, wife of Edward Boscawen, 87.
—— wife of William Evelyn, 135.
Glover, Col., 11.
Godstone, Surrey, 1, 4.
Gordon, Capt., allowed to visit Gen. Prescott, 101.
Gould, Edward, of Mansfield Woodhouse, 119.
—— Thoroton, Lieut. 4th Foot, 134; wounded, 55; biographical account, 119—121; his declaration concerning the battles of Lexington and Concord, 121, 122; examined on the trial of Horne Tooke, 124, 125.
—— Henry, succeeds to the Barony of Grey de Ruthyn, 120.
Gower, Mrs. Leveson, letters to her, 29, 31, 41, 63, 76; celebrated in Hannah More's poem, 132.
—— John Leveson, Admiral, 30, 134.
Granville, Bernard, letter to, 32.
—— Mary, (Mrs. Delany), letters to her, 33, 121.
Graves, Admiral, 77.
Grim, David, his record of the destruction of New York, 85.

Haines, Henry, 25.
Haldimand, Gen., 34.
Hamilton, David, Lieut. 4th Foot, 134.
Hancock, Col., his seat attacked, 47.
Harcourt, E. W. Vernon, of Nuneham, 30, 112.
—— Simon, Earl, 58, 103; account of his accident in Nuneham park, 110.
—— William, Lieut.-Col., captures General Lee, 103, 104; returns to England, 109; praised by King George III., 109; received the thanks of Parliament, 111.
Hay, John, Ensign, 4th Foot, 134.
Hildeburn, Charles R., owner of Inman's Journal, 14.
Hodgson, Studholme, Col. 4th Foot, 133.

INDEX.

Holmes, William, Capt. 4th Foot, 133.
Horne, John: see *Tooke, Horne.*
Howe, Sir William, 35, 113, 128; despatches, 9, 12; appointed commander of the English forces, 80.
Hunter, Martin, General, extract from his Journal, 62.
Hutchinson, George, Lieut. and Adjutant, 4th Foot, 126, 134.
Hyatt, Henry, Ensign, 4th Foot, 134.

Ingersoll, Jared, 36.
Ingraham, Duncan, 125, 126.
Inman, George, his MS. Journal quoted, 14.

James, G. P. R., 111.
Jefferson, Thomas, 41.
Johnson, Samuel, extracts from Boswell's Life of, 131—133; opinion of Blair's Sermons, 133.
Johnston, Henry P., extract from his account of the campaign around New York, 89.

Kelsey, Henry, 25.
King's Own Regiment, 4th Foot so called, 7; extract from its records, 13; muster-roll, 1774, 133, 134.
Knatchbull, John, 25.
Knight, Joseph, Lieut. 4th Foot, 91, 134; killed in action, 55, 59.
Knowles, Richard, Surgeon, 4th Foot, 134.

Langton, Bennett, extract from a letter to Boswell, 132.
Lee, Charles, General, 86; account of his capture by Col. Harcourt, 103—105, 114—117; his release demanded by Washington, 108; exchanged for General Prescott, 109; letter to General Gates, 117, 118.
Leonard, Daniel, author of "Massachusettensis," 49.
Leveson, John, 44.
Lexington, America, 8; battle of, 56, 119.
Livingstone, Col. Robert, a prisoner, 107.
Long Ditton, Surrey, 1, 20.
Lorimer, Hugh, 75.
—— James, 75.
Lossing, B. J., 111.

Ludgershall, Bucks, 3.
Lutterell, Henry, picture of the Evelyn family painted by him, 5.
Lyons, Capt., 75.

Maddison, George, Lieut.-Col., 133.
—— John Thomas, Ensign, 4th Foot, 134.
Marr, James, his affidavit, 126.
Massachusettensis: see *Leonard, Daniel.*
Matthews, General, 107.
Meade, Jane, wife of Richard Evelyn, 135.
Mickle, Isaac, author of "Reminiscences of Old Gloucester," 15.
Montague, Admiral George, note, 26.
Montresor, John, biographical note, 35.
More, Hannah, quotation from, 132.
Musgrave, Lieut.-Col., wounded, 10.
Myers, T. Baily, of New York, 95.

Napier, William, 61.
New York, 11, 83; one third destroyed by fire, 85, 86.
Nourse, Joseph, registrar of the Treasury, 113.
Novanglus, pseudonym of John Adams, 49.
Nuneham, Oxon, 103, 110.
—— Lord, letter to, 105.

Ogilvie, James, Major, 4th Foot, 133.
Oliphant, Mr., 43.
Oughton, Sir Adolphus, 43.
Owen, Dr., 4.
Oxfordshire Light Infantry, or 52nd Regiment, distinguished itself at the battle of Bunker's Hill, 61, 62.

Pattison, Col., supersedes Col. Cleaveland, 99, 100.
Percy, Hugh Earl, 57; biographical notes, 126—131.
Peter the Great occupies Say's Court, 1.
Pitcairn, John, Major, 52.
Plantagenet, Beauchamp, engaged by Sir Edmund Ployden to colonise his New Albion, 16, 17; prints a description of the colony, 17; arms, and grant of Belvedere, 18.
Ployden, Barbara, created Baroness of Richneck, 18.

Index

Ployden, Sir Edmund, obtains a grant of territory in the United States, 15; assumes the title of Earl Palatine, 16.
Potts, John, 94.
Preble, Jedidiah, his diary quoted, 57.
Prescott, Richard, Gen., 34, 42, 86; commands at Newport, 100; taken prisoner, *ib.*; account of the severity of his imprisonment, 101, 102; exchanged for Gen. Lee, 102.

Quebec, siege of, 102.

Ramsey, Allen, 131.
Rawdon, Lord, 78, 82.
Reynolds, Sir Joshua, 132.
Richards, Capt., 107.
Robertson, Dr., 131.
Rooke, Harry, Lieut. and Quartermaster, 4th Foot, 134.
Rupert, Prince, 2.
Russell, Thomas, Ensign, 4th Foot, 134.

Say's Court, Kent, residence of John Evelyn, 1.
Sewell, Jonathan, 49.
Shepherd, Col., 11.
Shuldham, Molyneux, Baron Shuldham, 77.
Smith, Francis, Lieut.-Col., 56.
Spenser, Edmund, quoted, 6.
St. Helen's, Isle of Wight, described, 27.
Staten Island, 9.
Steer, Mr., 43.
Stiles, Ezra, D.D., President of Yale College, his diary quoted, 10; biographical note, *ib.*
Stoughton, Thomas, marries Catherine Evelyn, 22.

Tangier Regiment, 4th Regiment, or King's Own, 7.

Thomlinson, Thomas, Capt. 4th Foot, 133.
Thorne, Peregrine Fra., Lieut. 4th Foot, 134.
Thoroton, Mary, wife of Edward Gould, 119.
—— Robert, of Screveton Hall, 119.
Ticonderoga, 72.
Tooke, Horne, notes of his trial and conviction, 119, 123, 124.
Trim, Ireland, 1, 135.
Tring, Hertfordshire, 109.
Truro, 87.

Vesey, Mr., 132.

Walpole, Horace, 87.
Walter, Sir William, obtains the Godstone estate, 21.
Warren, Joseph, 8.
Washington, George, 9; demands the release of Gen. Lee, 108.
Webster, John, Capt. 4th Foot, 133.
West, John, Capt. 4th Foot, 133.
Wilkes, John, 124.
Wilkinson, James, Gen., his account of the capture of Gen. Lee, 104, 114, 115; extract from his memoirs, 113.
Williams, Rose, marries George Evelyn, 20.
—— Thomas, 20.
Willoughby, Henry, Lord Middleton, 119.
Windsor, Berks, 7.
Wotton, Surrey, 1, 5, 20.
Wright, Peggie, 90.

Yale College, America, 10.
Yelverton, Barbara, wife of E. T. Gould, 120.
Young, Capt., 17.
Yung, Gregory, of Yorkshire, 21.
—— Susanna, wife of Robert Evelyn, 21.